CRUCIAL ISSUES IN AMERICAN GOVERNMENT
Jack R. Fraenkel
Series Editor

THE UNITED STATES IN WORLD AFFAIRS:

WHAT IS ITS ROLE?

Fran Pratt
Acton-Boxborough High School
Acton, Ma

ALLYN
AND
BACON,
INC.

Boston • Rockleigh, N.J. • Atlanta • Dallas • Belmont, Calif.

Library of Congress Catalog Card Number: 75-30216

1 2 3 4 5 6 7 8 9   84 83 82 81 80 79 78 77 76

PREFACE

The series, *Crucial Issues in American Government*, focuses on a number of social and political dilemmas which exist in American society today. Each book in the series presents a detailed, in-depth look at a problem of considerable concern to different individuals, groups, and governmental decision-makers in the United States. A major concern has been to make the study of these problems as interesting and exciting as possible. Each book, therefore, presents different types of source materials, as well as a variety of differing ideas and viewpoints on the particular issue under consideration.

After a short introductory chapter, the chapters which follow explore the various dimensions of the issue in some detail. A concerted effort has been made to avoid indicating or even implying, that there is any one "right" or "correct" way to view these issues, or that there is any single "answer" or "solution" that should be followed by the citizenry or those in government in order to deal with the problem which the issue pinpoints. Conclusions are not drawn for students, but instead, many open-ended questions are raised to promote careful thought and inquiry.

Each of the books in the series:

- presents a variety of divergent, and often conflicting, views on a social or political issue of considerable significance to many people in the United States and abroad;

- gives as many points of view on the issue as space permits;
- concentrates on the actions and feelings of real people involved with the issue;
- presents source material on a variety of reading levels:
- presents several subsidiary issues related to the problem under study so as to provide understanding in depth;
- presents illustrations, cartoons, photographs, and charts to help students obtain a total view of what the issue involves;
- includes a variety of open-ended questions and inquiry-oriented activities to stimulate analysis and investigation.

We hope that you enjoy the series.

JACK R. FRAENKEL
Series Editor

CONTENTS

ACKNOWLEDGEMENTS

MAPS, CHARTS, AND GRAPHS on the following pages were designed by GRAF-TECH: 17, 77, 92, 104, 108, 109.

CARTOONS, PHOTOS

8	Library of Congress
12	Allyn and Bacon, Inc. photo files
13	Library of Congress
14	Culver Pictures, Inc. (from the *Utica Saturday Globe*, 1899)
24	Library of Congress
31	Wide World Photos
40	Wide World Photos
44	*Crocodile* (Moscow), 1947
45	© 1961 St. Louis *Post Dispatch*. Reproduced by courtesy of Bill Mauldin.
56	World Bank/United Nations
66	Official United States Air Force Photograph
67	Japan Tourist Association
73	Wide World Photos
75	*The Herblock Gallery* (Simon & Schuster, 1968)
82	LePelley in *The Christian Science Monitor* © 1966 TCPS
83	Copyright © 1973 *The Chicago Sun-Times*. Reproduced by courtesy of Wil-Jo Associates, Inc. and Bill Mauldin.
84	*Aviation Week and Space Technology*, January 28, 1974. Copyright by McGraw-Hill, Inc.
97	Don Wright, *The Miami News*.

INTRODUCTION

Nora had left no doubt in her parents' minds as to what she wanted for her birthday. She was not exactly surprised, but she was very pleased when she came downstairs that morning and found a new ten-speed bicycle parked in the living room with a birthday card attached to the handlebars. She had wanted that bike a long time.

Her mother looked pleased. After a few appropriate words of thanks and a very hasty breakfast, Nora wheeled the bike outside and took off down the street for a test run. This morning the mother had no complaint as she picked up Nora's plate and scraped uneaten bacon and eggs into the garbage disposal.

Even if Nora hadn't been riding a new bike, she probably would not have paid much attention to her familiar surroundings—the neat rows of upper middle class suburban homes with their well-kept lawns, the plastic barrels placed by the curb for the weekly trash pickup, a neighbor pushing an electric lawn mower, the late model cars and campers parked in driveways. As a large Air Force jet flew high overhead, Nora neither heard its distant roar nor noticed the white trails it traced across the sky. All these things had been seen so many times they were just taken for granted.

Living in the richest country in the world, there was no reason for Nora to think of these common sights as symbolizing the vast wealth and power of the United States. Yet they do.

On this morning (or any other morning) that Nora decided to forego a full breakfast because she had better things to do, there were millions of people in places with exotic names like Bangladesh, Mauritania, and Haiti who would be astonished at the thought of turning down something to eat. Like most of her friends, Nora had never seen the city dump to which the contents of those plastic barrels were carried every week. Even if she had, she probably would not have been impressed by the fact that Americans throw out over 150 million tons of trash every year and pay more than $3 billion to have it disposed of.[1]

Nora might have been impressed, however, if she knew that her new bicycle cost more than the average person's income for an entire year in Ethiopia, Burma, or Afghanistan. She might also have been impressed if she knew that the jet flying high overhead—one of more than 400 such long-range bombers assigned to the Strategic Air Command—was carrying a single thermonuclear bomb with more explosive power than *all* of the explosives set off by *all* nations in *all* of World War II.

When Nora's neighbor flipped the switch to start his electric mower, he was tapping into a power network that generates one-third of all the electric power in the world to serve only six percent of the world's people. As one of those shiny new automobiles rolls out of a driveway, the driver may choose from more than three million miles of roads and highways to go anywhere in the United States. Keeping all those cars rolling takes a lot of gasoline, and Americans produce more of it than any other country. Yet they have to import oil to meet the nation's needs. The annual sales of the nation's largest automobile manufacturer, General Motors, exceed the entire production of all goods and services in 130 other nations.

Nora never knew specifically where the money came from to pay for her ten-speed bicycle or anything else her family had.

---

[1] Frequently statistics in this book will be expressed in "millions" and "billions." Keep in mind that *one million* means one thousand times one thousand (1000 × 1000). *One billion* is one thousand times one million (1000 × 1000 × 1000). Since it is so difficult to picture a billion of anything, here are two illustrations that may help. If you were given one billion dollars on the understanding that you would spend $1000 per day, you would have to live more than 2,700 years to spend it all. Another way of putting it is to imagine this book with one billion pages. With that many pages, this book would be almost as tall as two Empire State Buildings, one above the other.

She knew only that her father worked for a big company that frequently sent him on errands to other parts of the United States and, occasionally, to foreign countries. In fact, her father was a sales representative for a large corporation with overseas divisions in thirty-eight other countries. These American-based "multinational" corporations together account for more than half of all the foreign business investment in the world. When their boards of directors make policy decisions, in effect they decide not only whether Nora's father will be able to buy her a ten-speed bike, but whether people in dozens of other countries will even have a job.

One of the criteria used by economists to measure the economic status of a country is *gross national product* (GNP), which is defined as the total value of all goods and services produced by a nation in one year. GNP becomes more meaningful when it is divided into *per capita GNP*, or the average share of goods and services produced for each person. An editorial in *The New Republic* questions whether Americans, who have the highest per capita GNP in the world, are using their wealth wisely.

> It ill behooves a nation that has a per capita gross national product of $5530 to grumble or to pity itself. . . .
>
> We are social wastrels [wasters], spending $2.7 billion a year on air-conditioning—roughly the combined gross national products of Bolivia, Congo, Liberia, Haiti, and Guinea. . . . What can be said of our sense of proportion when gross sales of the US tobacco industry are roughly the same as our public investment in higher education—close to $14 billion a year. Consider also our excessive expenditure in fiscal '73 of $17.5 billion for offensive and defensive strategic nuclear forces which, if ever used, would guarantee mutual annihilation. And consider the estimate of a Brookings Institution staff report that projects an expenditure on these forces between now and 1980 of $160 billion. How much security is there in spending more and more for a big stick that can never be swung? We paid out $9.7 billion in 1972—slightly less than the gross national product of New Zealand—on canned and frozen foods, neither of which was known to Americans a century ago. We trade in our cars as if they were box tops, an estimated 4.1 million trade-ins annually. The kitchen towel, usable again and again, may soon become obsolete: about a third of a billion dollars a year are spent on paper towels for the home. . . . Or contemplate the $17.5 billion Americans

spend annually for over four billion gallons of beer, wine and hard liquors—more than one-fourth of India's GNP—and India has over two and a-half times our population.[2]

Living in America, it is difficult to appreciate the immense wealth and power of the United States. Like Nora, we all tend to take things for granted. Occasionally, a special program on television or a pictorial article in a news magazine may remind us of different worlds where life is not so kind. But so what? Not everyone can be rich and powerful, and Americans work hard for what they have. Even in this country there are poor people who need help. Until they are taken care of, why should America be concerned about the rest of the world?

In this book we will examine America's use of its wealth and power since World War II. We will begin in the first chapter by examining how the United States, traditionally an "isolationist" country, came to be involved in a variety of ways with the affairs of people around the world. Following chapters will deal with specific case studies of American involvement in foreign affairs. Throughout this book, there are three key questions you should be concerned with:

1. What responsibilities does the United States, as the world's richest and most powerful nation, have toward other nations?
2. Is the United States meeting its global responsibilities?
3. What should be the future direction of American policy toward the other peoples of the world?

These are not easy questions, and there are probably no "right" answers. They have been hotly debated by people here and abroad, by old and young, by those who pay taxes and those who decide what to use taxes for. They will continue to be debated as long as the United States holds its privileged position of wealth and power. This book will carry you into this debate and provide some basis by which you can draw your own conclusions about America's responsibilities and how they should be met.

---

[2] From "Wastrel of the Western World," *The New Republic*, January 5 and 12, 1974, p. 6. Reprinted by permission of the New Republic, © 1974 The New Republic, Inc.

THE MAKING OF A SUPERPOWER

The rise of the United States from a few scattered settlements strung out along the Atlantic coast to the "superpower" of the twentieth century is a story unique in the history of nations. The immigrants who came to the "New World" from Europe found a continent over 3000 miles wide, brimming with natural resources, and sparsely inhabited by people whom the settlers called "Indians." Located in the temperate zone with a generally moderate climate, North America had the makings of a rich country right from the start. Vast expanses of fertile land, giant forests, abundant rivers and lakes, and a variety of mineral resources all lay waiting. All that was needed was time, labor, and capital to make it productive.

Starting with the early seventeenth-century English colonies along the Atlantic Coast, the process of development took almost three centuries until the frontier was officially declared closed in the 1890s. By that time the countryside from Atlantic to Pacific was dotted with communities containing homes, schools, churches, factories, and meeting houses. Roads, railroads, and canals were connected with natural waterways to tie the whole vast expanse together. Through wars, treaties, and occupation, huge territories had been taken from Mexico and withheld from others who claimed the land. The tragic Indian wars had drawn to a close with the surviving native Americans pushed back onto desolate reservations of poor land that nobody else wanted.

In the latter half of the nineteenth century industry grew rapidly. From the election of Abraham Lincoln (1860) to the outbreak of World War I (1914) the value of American manufactures rose from $2 billion to $24 billion. By 1894 the United States had already become the world's foremost industrial power, and by 1914 it was manufacturing industrial products worth more than the combined industrial output of its three closest competitors—Great Britain, France, and Germany.

The labor and capital to make all of this possible came largely from Europe. At first population grew slowly, but by the second half of the nineteenth century immigrants were flocking to America—eventually more than one million per year. Most of the immigrants brought with them their life savings. Many other wealthy Europeans, who had no cause to leave their homelands, sent millions of dollars for investment in the growth of American business and industry. During the nineteenth century, the United States was a "debtor nation," owing more to foreign countries (especially England) than foreigners owed to it. Early in the twentieth century, the situation began to be reversed. By the time of World War I, Wall Street in New York had replaced Bond Street in London as the financial capital of the world. It would be no exaggeration to say that early in the twentieth century the United States became, in economic terms, the world's strongest nation.

This chapter reviews the growth of American power and influence in world affairs. It begins with a time when the country had little interest in foreign affairs, and concludes with a time when the United States is involved in all parts of the world. There are two basic views as to how this happened.

As you read the chapter, make your own analysis of this issue by making a set of notes in two columns listing evidence that would support each of the following views. When you finish the chapter, examine the two columns, draw your own conclusions, and discuss the results with other members of your class.

1. The United States was forced into a position of world leadership by events over which it had little control. Americans did not seek world power, but were forced to exercise power to protect their own freedom and security.

2. Americans are naturally aggressive and have actively tried to control the affairs of other people. On its own initiative, the United States has taken actions and pursued policies which have led to world leadership.

★ MOVING FROM ISOLATIONISM

It is one thing to be "leader of the world" in the statistical sense of producing more bushels of wheat, manufacturing more yards of textiles, and having more dollars to loan than any other nation. It is a much different thing to exercise "world leadership," that is, to assume the responsibility for consciously using this power and influence to determine not only one's own destiny, but the fate of other peoples as well. The first half of the twentieth century would see the United States emerge in the role of world leader. In order for this to happen, it was necessary that America's long standing commitment to a policy (or non-policy) of isolationism be abandoned.

It seems only natural that throughout the nineteenth century America's attention was ordinarily focused inward upon itself. So long as there were forests to be cleared, plains to be settled, railroads to be built, and Mexicans to be fought, Americans had neither the energy nor the desire to become entangled in foreign problems. The country was generally disinterested and unconcerned with the affairs of the rest of the world—the Americans were busy building their nation.

Historians have fallen into the habit of using the term *isolationism* to describe this long period of America's non-involvement in foreign affairs. Of course, pure isolation was impossible. For trade purposes, if for no other reason, the government found it necessary to negotiate treaties with foreign powers and to maintain a navy to protect American ships on the high seas. Sometimes American troops found themselves in combat with foreign armed forces, as they did in the War of 1812 and the Mexican War (1846–1848). But from the American point of view, these conflicts had more to do with territorial expansion and the internal needs of the country than they did with any foreign cause. It was not until the end of the century that American forces were sent to fight "somebody else's battle" on foreign soil. The occasion was the Spanish-American War.

As you read the following pages describing the Spanish-American War and the building of an American empire, make your own judgment about the character of America's role. Below is a list of terms one might use, depending on viewpoint, to describe the United States in this era. Choose the term which you think *best* characterizes the United States at that time, and make a list of evidence you could use to support your position. Discuss your viewpoint with your classmates.

peace maker
policing agent
imperialist
humanitarian

foolish giant
bully
warmonger
defender of freedom

$50,000 REWARD.—WHO DESTROYED THE MAINE?—$50,000 REWARD

EDITION FOR GREATER NEW YORK

NEW YORK JOURNAL
AND ADVERTISER.

The Journal will give $50,000 for information, furnished to it exclusively, that will convict the person or persons who sank the Maine.

The Journal will give $50,000 for information, furnished to it exclusively, that will convict the person or persons who sank the Maine.

NO. 3,572. NEW YORK, THURSDAY, FEBRUARY 17, 1898.—16 PAGES. PRICE ONE CENT

DESTRUCTION OF THE WAR SHIP MAINE WAS THE WORK OF AN ENEMY

$50,000!
$50,000 REWARD!
For the Detection of the Perpetrator of the Maine Outrage!

FOR THE PERPETRATOR OF THIS OUTRAGE HAD ACCOMPLICES.

Assistant Secretary Roosevelt Convinced the Explosion of the War Ship Was Not an Accident.

The Journal Offers $50,000 Reward for the Conviction of the Criminals Who Sent 258 American Sailors to Their Death. Naval Officers Unanimous That the Ship Was Destroyed on Purpose.

$50,000!
$50,000 REWARD
For the Detection of the Perpetrator of the Maine Outrage!

FOR THE PERPETRATOR OF THIS OUTRAGE HAD ACCOMPLICES.

NAVAL OFFICERS THINK THE MAINE WAS DESTROYED BY A SPANISH MINE.

Hidden Mine or a Sunken Torpedo Believed to Have Been the Weapon Used Against the American Man-of-War---Officers and Men Tell Thrilling Stories of Being Blown Into the Air Amid a Mass of Shattered Steel and Exploding Shells---Survivors Brought to Key West Scout the Idea of Accident---Spanish Officials Protest Too Much---Our Cabinet Orders a Searching Inquiry---Journal Sends Divers to Havana to Report Upon the Condition of the Wreck. Was the Vessel Anchored Over a Mine?

BY CAPTAIN E. L. ZALINSKI, U. S. A.

Assistant Secretary of the Navy Theodore Roosevelt says he is convinced that the destruction of the Maine in Havana Harbor was not an accident. The Journal offers a reward of $50,000 for exclusive evidence that will convict the person, persons or Government criminally responsible for the destruction of the American battle ship and the death of 258 of its crew.

The suspicion that the Maine was deliberately blown up grows stronger every hour. Not a single fact to the contrary has been produced. Captain Sigsbee, of the Maine, and Consul-General Lee both urge that public opinion be suspended until they have completed their inquiry. They are taking the course of tactful men who are convinced that there has been treachery.

The United States entered the war with Spain in 1898. By that time fighting had been going on for three years on the island of Cuba, just ninety miles from the tip of Florida. The American press had been giving extensive coverage to the Cuban revolt with special emphasis on charges of cruelty and atrocities committed by the Spanish authorities on the island who were trying to suppress the revolt and hold on to the little that remained of Spain's once vast empire in Latin America.

Until 1898, the United States took an officially neutral position. However, there was strong sympathy among Americans for the Cuban rebels, and many favored American intervention. "War fever" was greatly increased in February when the American battleship *Maine* exploded and sank in the Cuban port of Havana. Two hundred sixty American seamen went down with the ship. In spite of an official inquiry that cleared the Spanish of responsibility for the explosion, it was widely assumed that Spain was to blame.

Examine the photograph (opposite) showing the front page of the *New York Journal* announcing the sinking of the *Maine*. Consider the following questions:

1. Does the newspaper tell who was responsible for sinking the *Maine?*
2. Does the newspaper imply that anyone in particular was responsible for sinking the *Maine?*
3. Why would a newspaper offer a reward such as the one advertised in this newspaper?
4. What effect do you think news headlines like these would have on public opinion toward going to war? Why?

On April 11, 1898, President William McKinley outlined for Congress the alternatives for the United States. Without specifically requesting a declaration of war, he made a strong case for military intervention. Eight days later, Congress approved a joint resolution authorizing the president to use the armed forces to see that Spain "at once relinquish [give up] its authority and government in the Island of Cuba and withdraw its land and naval forces from Cuba and Cuban waters." According to the resolution, the United States made these demands because "the people of Cuba are, and of right ought to be, free and independent." McKinley summarized for Congress the grounds for intervention as follows:

First. In the cause of humanity and to put an end to the barbarities, bloodshed, starvation, and horrible miseries now existing there, and which the parties to the conflict are either unable or unwilling to stop or mitigate [lessen]. It is no answer to say that this is all in another country, belonging to another nation, and is, therefore, none of our business. It is specially our duty, for it is right at our door.

Second. We owe it to our citizens in Cuba to afford them that protection . . . for life and property which no government there can or will afford, and to that end to terminate [end] the conditions that deprive them of legal protection.

Third. The right to intervene may be justified by the very serious injury to the commerce, trade, and business of our people and by the wanton destruction of property and devastation of the island.

Fourth, and which is of utmost importance. The present condition of affairs in Cuba is a constant menace to our peace and entails upon this government an enormous expense. With such a conflict waged for years in an island so near us and with which our people have such trade and business relations; when the lives and liberties of our citizens are in constant danger and their property destroyed and themselves ruined; where our trading vessels are liable to seizure and are seized at our very door by warships of a foreign nation; . . . all these and others which I need not mention . . . are a constant menace to our peace and compel us to keep on a semi-war footing with a nation with which we are at peace. . . .

In view of these facts and of these considerations I ask the Congress to authorize and empower the President to take measures to secure a full and final termination of hostilities between the government of Spain and the people of Cuba, and to secure in the island the establishment of a stable government, capable of maintaining order and observing its international obligations, ensuring peace and tranquillity and the security of its citizens as well as our own, and to use the military and naval forces of the United States as may be necessary for these purposes.

---

1. Examine each of the arguments put forth by President McKinley for United States intervention in Cuba. Which of the following, if

any, do you think would be a reasonable basis for the United States to go to war?

   a. To protect citizens of another country from "barbarities, bloodshed, starvation, and horrible miseries."
   b. To protect American citizens in a foreign country when their "life and property" are endangered.
   c. To protect the "commerce, trade, and business of our people" from "wanton destruction."
   d. To keep peace in another country close to our own.

2. On the basis of McKinley's arguments, would you agree that the United States had a "right" to intervene? A "duty"? Why or why not?

Historians offer a variety of interpretations of American involvement in the war with Spain. One popular theory is that, as the frontier on the mainland closed, ambitious business and political leaders began to look toward the rich and fertile islands of the Caribbean as the logical next step for American expansion. The confident, yet unfulfilled, mood of America on the eve of the war has been well described by the historian, Hubert Herring. As you read this selection, see what you can add to your understanding of American involvement.

A new mood had laid its spell upon the Americans of the north. It was a mood born, in part, of an exultant sense of power: the smokestacks were belching clouds of smoke and flame, and thousands of factories, mills, and plants were turning out everything from carpet tacks to locomotives. The United States, men said, had everything: the finest of manpower from England, Germany, Scandinavia, and all of Europe; soil for raising every crop and for the pasturing of herds; mines with vast reserves; wells tapping lakes of petroleum. Yet with all this treasure, there was a sense of inadequacy. The land had been staked out from Maine to California; cities and towns were growing unwieldly; a great population (about 69,000,000 in 1895) was crowding this fruitful land. Gloomy prophets said that shortly there would be too many people, too great an industrial output, and an inadequate market. The United States—they said—must enter the lists of empire, capture new lands and markets. The British, French, Italians, and Russians had already extended

their lines; the Germans and Japanese were following their
example; the Americans could not be left behind.[1]

Compare the photographs of a frontier town in Montana (below) and
the Eastside of New York City (opposite) with Hubert Herring's
description of America in the late nineteenth century.

1. What passages can you find in the selection by Hubert Herring
   that are illustrated in the photos?
2. Can you see anything in the photos that might help to explain why
   the United States at that time would start to be more interested in
   what was happening outside of the country?
3. Do you think the people in the frontier town in Montana or the
   people of the Eastside would be most interested in foreign affairs
   like the situation in Cuba? Why?

[1] Hubert Herring, *A History of Latin America*, 2d ed., (New York: Alfred A.
Knopf, 1964) p. 798.

The war was not confined strictly to the island of Cuba, nor even to the Caribbean, but involved Spain's Pacific empire as well. In both the Caribbean and Pacific theaters Spain's defeat on land and sea came swiftly. In 1895 Theodore Roosevelt had written to Senator Henry Cabot Lodge saying, "This country needs a war." In the same spirit, when the war was over, Secretary of State John Hay wrote to Roosevelt saying, "It has been a splendid little war." As the "splended little war" came to a close, it was evident that the United States had proved itself capable of fighting and winning naval battles on two oceans at the same time. No longer could any country lightly regard the power of the United States.

Besides whatever military prestige was gained by the war with Spain, the United States also acquired an empire. As you read the following selection, note the stages of growth in the appetite of the McKinley administration for the control of overseas territories.

The United States clearly had no territorial ambitions at the outbreak of the war. Congress' war resolution had stated that

Cuba ought to be free and independent, and if Spain failed to grant independence instantly McKinley might use the armed forces of the United States to win Cuba's freedom from Spain. Then followed a fateful amendment, offered by Senator Henry M. Teller of Colorado, that the United States pledge herself to leave Cuba in control of the Cuban people.

While the war with Spain was in progress, American policy toward the acquisition of territory began to change. On July 6, 1898, Congress adopted a joint resolution annexing Hawaii to the United States. Two weeks later, in stating terms for an armistice in the war, McKinley demanded the cession [surrender] of Puerto Rico and of Guam. He stipulated, moreover, that the United States was to occupy the "city, bay, and harbor of Manila pending the conclusion of a treaty of peace." "By our code of morality," McKinley had said earlier, annexation of territory "would be criminal aggression." By July, along with the rest of the country, he was becoming less abstemious [sparing]. "We must keep all we get," he said; "when the war is over, we must keep what we want."

While America's negotiators were preparing to make the treaty with Spain, American hunger for the Philippines kept growing. First it was only Manila; then, on September 16, the

Uncle Sam is saying to Aguinaldo, "Come inside young rascal; I'm tired of chasing you around in the wet." What does he mean by this remark? What evidence in the McKinley administration article can you find to support your ideas?

negotiators were instructed by McKinley to take nothing less than the island of Luzon. By October 26, the whole archipelago [chain of islands] was being demanded. When Spain demurred [hesitated], an ultimatum [final demand] was issued on November 21, to which Spain capitulated [gave in]. "There was nothing left for us to do," the President explained to a group of Methodist ministers later, "but to take them all, and civilize and Christianize them, and by God's grace to do the very best we could by them as our fellow men for whom Christ also died.". . .

On February 6, 1899, the Senate narrowly ratified the treaty by 57–27 — only two votes above the required two-thirds. The decision was influenced by the reaction of the Filipinos themselves. For on December 21, 1898, while the debate in the Senate was at its peak, McKinley had ordered the War Department to extend the military occupation of Manila to the entire Philippines. This move served to touch off a Filipino insurrection [revolt], which promptly took the lives of American soldiers and no doubt swayed Senate votes. The insurrection, led by Emilio Aguinaldo, lasted three sordid years and cost more than the war with Spain itself. Before it was put down, American forces had to resort to the same concentration camp methods that the Spanish had used to combat the guerillas in Cuba. Thus a movement that had started as an effort to liberate the Cubans ended in a drive to subjugate the Filipinos.

Nor, indeed, were the Cubans actually liberated. General Wood remained in Cuba as military governor until May 20, 1902, and then Cuba was forced to subscribe to the so-called Platt Amendment.[2] General Wood accomplished important reforms: he inaugurated an excellent sanitation program, set up a school system, rebuilt Havana, put the island's finances on a stable basis, and kept peace while a convention sat to draw up Cuba's new constitution. The General's presence in

---

[2] The "Platt Amendment" was added to an appropriations bill for the U.S. Army. The amendment placed a number of restrictions on Cuba's independence by limiting its right to make treaties, borrow money from foreign countries, and control many of its own affairs. It also guaranteed the right of the United States to have a naval base in Cuba and allowed the United States to intervene in Cuba whenever life and property were threatened. In the 1930s these American rights over Cuba were given up as part of President Roosevelt's "Good Neighbor Policy," but even today the United States continues to maintain a naval base at Guantanamo Bay.

Cuba gradually became suspect, but the United States, despite the Teller Amendment, was not yet prepared to yield the islands fully.[3]

In the years following the Spanish-American War, the United States gained a number of overseas possessions by purchase, by treaty, and by annexation. Study the map showing the United States Overseas Possessions acquired prior to 1935, and consider the following questions.

1. When were the first overseas possessions acquired by the United States? What territories were they?
2. How much of the American empire was acquired in the two decades following the Spanish-American War?
3. How do you think the growth of this empire affected the United States in regard to each of the following? Why?

   a. Interest in foreign affairs
   b. Foreign trade
   c. Available resources for industry
   d. The size of the army and navy
   e. Amount of taxes Americans paid

★ A NEW AMERICAN IMAGE

The Spanish-American War gave the United States a new identity in the world, and it also gave Americans a new image of themselves. Some liked the new image; others did not. We can generally refer to these opposing groups as "imperialists" and "anti-imperialists." For the next several years, their debate was one of the hottest issues around which American politics revolved.

The war gave the United States an empire. Americans were accustomed to the expansion of territory; but this expansion was different. The territories were overseas, sometimes thousands of miles away. And they were heavily populated. Until this time, it had been assumed that new territory would serve to enlarge the Union. As territories were added, they were settled by Ameri-

---

[3] From *The United States: The History of a Republic* by Richard Hofstadter, William Miller, and Daniel Aaron. (Englewood Cliffs, N.J.: Prentice-Hall, Inc., 1957), pp. 562–564. Reprinted by permission of the publisher.

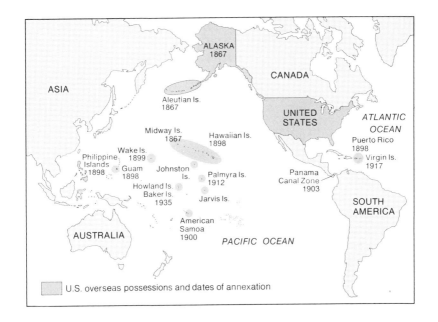

cans and, when sufficiently developed, were added to the Union as states. Following the Constitution, new states had the same rights and responsibilities as the original thirteen. It now became apparent to anti-imperialists that the government did not regard places like Puerto Rico, Hawaii, and the Philippines in the same way. These were "foreign possessions" to be ruled by the United States, not candidates for statehood entitled to the same rights of self-government as the states on the mainland. No longer did the Constitution follow the flag.

Anti-imperialists asked how the United States, with its traditions of democracy and freedom, could justify the domination of millions of unwilling subjects overseas. Albert J. Beveridge, senator from Indiana, justified America's new role this way:

> God has marked the American people as His chosen nation to finally lead in the regeneration [rebirth] of the world. This is the divine mission of America, and it holds for us all the profit, all the glory, all the happiness possible to man. We are trustees of the world's progress, guardians of its righteous peace.

The following two readings will give you some insight into the nature of the debate over imperialism. The first reading presents selections from an address made in 1900 by Elihu Root, who was Secretary of War during the Spanish-American conflict. The anti-imperialist viewpoint is stated by William Jennings Bryan, the Democratic candidate for president that year. Which of the arguments do you find most convincing. Why?

The Imperialist Viewpoint

. . . Imperialism! The word has a familiar sound. The cry is one of the cheapest and most threadbare of the demagogue's [popular orator's] stock, always certain to produce a sensation among a people alert to the protection of their liberties. Jefferson was denounced as an imperialist; Lincoln was denounced as an imperialist; Grant was denounced as an imperialist; and to all three of these great and liberty-loving men the party of opposition made the country resound with loud campaign outcries that they were about to strangle the liberties of the country by force, just as they are now clamoring against President McKinley. Is there any more in the cry now than there were in the days of Jefferson, of Lincoln, and of Grant? Is the character of our institutions really about to be changed, or are our liberties really in danger? Is the issue substantial, or is it but the demagogue's cry? . . .

Nothing can be more misleading than a principle misapplied. Countless crimes have been committed by men quoting texts of Scripture or maxims of political philosophy wrested from their true context and meaning. The doctrine that government derives its just powers from the consent of the governed was applicable to the conditions for which Jefferson wrote it, and to the people to whom he applied it. It is true wherever a people exist capable and willing to maintain just government, and to make free, intelligent and efficacious [effective] decision as to who shall govern. But Jefferson did not apply it to Louisiana. He wrote to Gallatin that the people of Louisiana were as incapable of self-government as children, and he governed them without their consent. Lincoln did not apply it to the South, and the great struggle of the Civil War was a solemn assertion by the American people that there are other principles of law and liberty which limit the application of the doctrine of consent. The immutable [unchangeable] laws of justice and humanity require that people shall have government . . . whether there be consent or not. . . .

The true question in the Philippines was, whether the withdrawal of the Spanish power which we had destroyed left a people capable of establishing and maintaining a free constitutional government; whether the humble and peaceable inhabitants, who constituted the great mass of the population, were competent to protect themselves . . . or whether, on the other hand, the people, incapable of governing themselves, would become the subjects of a dictatorship . . . .

The testimony is absolutely overwhelming that the people inhabiting the Philippine Archipelago are incapable of self-government. . . . There is no Philippine people. The hundreds of islands which compose the Archipelago are inhabited by more than eighty different tribes, speaking more than sixty different languages. They have no common medium of communication, and they never had a government except the arbitrary rule of Spain. Most of them have not the first conception of what self-government means, or the first qualification for its exercise. Many of them have the capacity to learn, but they have never learned.[4]

The Anti-Imperialist Viewpoint

. . . for more than a century this nation has been a world power, but it has done more to shape the politics of the human race than all the other nations of the world combined. Because our Declaration of Independence was promulgated [announced] others have been promulgated. Because the patriots of 1776 fought for liberty others have fought for it. Because our Constitution was adopted other constitutions have been adopted.

The growth of the principle of self-government planted on American soil, has been the overshadowing political fact of the nineteenth century. It has made this nation conspicuous among the nations and given it a place in history such as no other nation has ever enjoyed. Nothing has been able to check the onward march of this idea. I am not willing that this nation shall cast aside the omnipotent [all powerful] weapon of truth to seize again the weapons of physical warfare. I would not exchange the glory of this Republic for the glory of all the empires that have risen and fallen since time began. . . .

---

[4]   From *The Military and Colonial Policy of the United States: Addresses and Reports by Elihu Root* by Robert Bacon and James Brown Scott (eds.). (Cambridge, Mass.: Harvard University Press, 1916.), pp. 34–50 *passim.* Reprinted by permission of the publisher.

The permanent chairman of the last Republican National convention presented the . . . argument in all its baldness when he said:

"We make no hypocritical pretense of being interested in the Philippines solely on account of others. While we regard the welfare of those people as a sacred trust, we regard the welfare of the American people first. We see our duty to ourselves as well as to others. We believe in trade expansion. By every legitimate means within the province of government and constitution we mean to stimulate the expansion of our trade and open new markets." . . .

It is not necessary to own people in order to trade with them. We carry on trade today with every part of the world, and our commerce has expanded more rapidly than the commerce of any European empire. . . . Trade cannot be permanently profitable unless it is voluntary.

When trade is secured by force, the cost of securing it and retaining it must be taken out of the profits, and the profits are never large enough to cover the expense. Such a system would never be defended but for the fact that the expense is borne by all the people, while the profits are enjoyed by a few. . . .

. . . I can conceive of a national destiny surpassing the glories of the present and the past—a destiny which meets the responsibilities of today and measures up to the possibilities of the future. Behold a republic, *resting securely upon the foundation stones quarried by revolutionary patriots from the mountain of eternal truth*—a republic applying in practice and proclaiming to all the world the self-evident propositions that all men are created equal; that they are endowed by their Creator with inalienable rights; that governments are instituted among men to secure these rights, and that governments derive their just powers from the consent of the governed. . . . Behold a republic standing erect while empires all around are bowed beneath the weight of their own armaments—a republic whose flag is loved while other flags are only feared . . . a republic whose history, like the path of the just "is as the shining light that shineth more and more unto the perfect day."[5]

---

[5] From *Speeches of William Jennings Bryan*. Published by Funk & Wagnalls Publishing Company, Inc., 1909, pp. 39–49 *passim*.

The controversy over imperialism reflected an even more basic division in American thinking. On one hand were the isolationists who felt that America's success was somehow tied in to her ability to steer clear of other people's problems. With the Atlantic on one side, the Pacific on the other, and all that good land in between, who needed friends or enemies in Europe and Asia? Who needed an empire? Opposed to these isolationists, on the other hand, was a growing number of people who found it more and more difficult to distinguish between the interests of America and the interests of the world. For these people, foreign problems were no longer "foreign."

1. Examine the following statements and try to associate them with the preceding speeches for and against imperialism. Which statements do you think would be approved by Elihu Root? By William Jennings Bryan? By neither? By both? Find passages in their speeches that you think support your answers.

   a. Law and order are more important than freedom.
   b. In world affairs, the main concern of the United States should be to look out for itself.
   c. Being self-sufficient, the United States doesn't need to trade with foreigners.
   d. American influence in the world is not so much a matter of what Americans "believe" as it is of what they do.
   e. All people are capable of governing themselves.
   f. The United States should not concern itself with being a "world power."

2. Does "anti-imperialism" mean the same thing as "isolationism"? What evidence can you find in the speeches to support your answer?

3. With which of the statements listed above do you agree or disagree? Why?

★ TOWARD GLOBAL INVOLVEMENT

The Spanish-American War marked a trend away from isolationism, but by no means did isolationist feelings die. As American interests around the world continued to grow through the twentieth century, many Americans continued to hold a strong desire to stay out of other people's problems.

There was not a single word about foreign affairs in the inaugural address given by Woodrow Wilson in 1913. When World War I began the following year, the government immediately adopted an officially neutral position. The war in Europe had been going on for more than two years when Wilson won reelection in 1916 on the slogan: "He kept us out of war." Although the United States was the chief supplier of the "Allies" fighting against Germany and Austria, it was not until three years after the war began that the first American "doughboys" arrived on the battlefields of Europe.

The fact that American soldiers were not dying on European battlefields before 1917 does not mean that Americans were unconcerned with what was going on. Just as spectators at a football game cannot remain uninvolved, Americans took sides. Most Americans supported the Allies, especially Britain and France, for a variety of reasons. For one thing, Americans felt a closer bond toward the relatively democratic governments of those two countries than they did to the undemocratic monarchies of Germany and Austria. The conflict was widely interpreted as a contest between democracy and dictatorship. Britain skillfully manipulated the news arriving from Europe to encourage this view of the war. Since most of the news arriving in America came through the British-controlled transoceanic telegraph cables, the British were able to manage the news to their own advantage.

Although American businesses were legally free to sell war materiel and other supplies to either side, the British maintained a naval blockade of the continent that kept goods from getting to their enemies. As war-related industry boomed in the United States, the country developed a financial stake in the outcome of the war. After 1915, most of the sales to the Allies were done on a credit basis. Many came to believe that the United States could not afford to see the Allies lose since they owed so much money to American creditors.

Germany's answer to the British naval blockade was the submarine. British propaganda pictured the submarine, with its silent and unannounced torpedo attacks, as a hideous instrument of war that was unworthy of any civilized people. The sinking of the British liner *Lusitania* in May 1915, brought death to almost 1,200 people who were unaware that war materiel was included in the ship's cargo. Although the German embassy had warned Americans against traveling on Allied ships, the American public was enraged over the death of 128 American citizens who went down with the ship.

The United States government protested to Germany and threatened to enter the war. Germany, pointing out that Britain was guilty of her own violations of the rules of the sea, agreed to halt submarine attacks on nonmilitary vessels. But as the British blockade continued, and American supplies continued to pour into Allied ports, the Germans finally resumed unrestricted submarine warfare.

Five American ships were sunk in March 1917. On April 2, Wilson asked Congress for a declaration of war to help make the world "safe for democracy." Four days later, by a vote of 373 to 50 in the House of Representatives and 82 to 6 in the Senate, the declaration of war was passed. Within a few months, American troops were arriving in Europe, and by October they were involved in combat. At home and abroad the cause of war rapidly took on all the enthusiasm of a crusade.

Just as the sinking of the *Maine* played an important part in bringing the United States into the war with Spain, the sinking of ships by German submarines was an important factor in American entry into World War I. Compare the photos showing the front pages of newspapers announcing the sinking of the *Lusitania* (page 24) and the *Maine* (page 8).

1. Which of the two announcements do you think would be most likely to influence public opinion in favor of war? Why?
2. Do you find any evidence of bias for or against war in the way the news was reported? Explain.
3. What difference, if any, do you think it would make to Americans that one ship (the *Maine*) was a U.S. battleship carrying military personnel while the other ship (the *Lusitania*) was a British ship carrying civilian passengers, some of whom were Americans? Should this make a difference? Why or why not?

In a little more than a year of fighting, the United States Army suffered more than 275,000 casualties. The direct cost of the war for the United States was eventually set at more than $22 billion. In spite of the massive investment of American life and money, the isolationist mood quickly came back to life when the war ended. As soon as the armistice was signed in November 1918 and the big guns became silent, the cry was raised to

"bring the boys home." The government lost no time in responding to public pressure, and within a few months all American forces were withdrawn from Europe.

Considering how frequently recent presidents travel abroad to engage in personal diplomacy, it now seems strange that Wilson was criticized for journeying to France to participate in the peace conference at Versailles. No other president had traveled abroad while in office, and Wilson's opponents capitalized on his "desertion" of the country. His critics claimed that there were pressing postwar problems that required his attention at home. When Wilson did return, the Senate refused to ratify the treaty he had helped to draft.

The central issue in the debate over the treaty was the proposed League of Nations, which Wilson had worked hard to get the other Allies to establish. Like the United Nations of today, the League was to be an international organization dedicated to resolving problems between nations and maintaining the peace. Among the arguments of those who opposed the treaty was that membership in the League would place an international body above the United States Congress. This, according to the critics, could lead the country into war without any action by the Congress. On this ground, they said, ratification of the treaty would be unconstitutional.

The United States never became a member of the international peace organization its president had worked so hard to create. In fact, for some years after Wilson left office, the White House did not even respond to messages from the League's headquarters in Geneva, Switzerland. Most other nations of the world did join the League, but some withdrew in the 1930s as a series of new crises led toward World War II. Certainly one of the League's handicaps as it tried to cope with these new threats to world peace was the absence of the world's most wealthy and powerful nation.

When Franklin D. Roosevelt came to the presidency in 1933, foreign affairs were the least of concerns for Americans. The economic depression that gripped Europe in the aftermath of World War I eventually engulfed the United States as well. Compared to the war years, foreign trade had almost come to a standstill. Across America, machines were left unattended; the sky was clear above the smokestacks; and twelve million workers were unemployed. Millions lost their savings, their homes, their farms, their security.

In Europe, where economic conditions were even worse, dictators rose to power. Benito Mussolini in Italy and Adolph Hitler in Germany established totalitarian regimes and prepared to solve their countries' problems by war. In 1936 they joined in the Axis alliance. Japan, which had launched a program of military conquest in Asia, joined the Axis pact a few years later. In September 1939, the world was once again plunged into war as German armies poured across the frontiers of Poland.

Again the United States sought to stay out of the conflict. But two days after the attack on Poland, Roosevelt addressed the nation by radio. Declaring that "I hate war," and assuring that he would do everything possible to keep the United States out of the conflict, he nevertheless sought to awaken the country to the dangers of the international scene:

You must master at the outset a simple but unalterable fact in modern foreign relations. When peace has been broken anywhere, peace of all countries everywhere is in danger.

It is easy for you and me to shrug our shoulders and say that conflicts taking place thousands of miles from the continental United States . . . do not seriously affect the Americas — and that all the United States has to do is to ignore them and go about our own business. Passionately though we may desire detachment, we are forced to realize that every word that comes through the air, every ship that sails the sea, every battle that is fought does affect the American future.

As in World War I, the United States became the "arsenal of democracy" furnishing massive quantities of aid to the Allies, but remaining out of direct combat. On December 7, 1941, a day called by Roosevelt a "day of infamy," the Japanese made a surprise attack on the American naval base at Pearl Harbor in Hawaii. More than 2,000 military personnel and civilians were killed. About 200 airplanes were destroyed, and 19 ships were either badly damaged or sunk. The next day, with only one opposing vote, Congress declared war. The *Chicago Tribune,* hitherto one of the main advocates for isolationism, now spoke for the whole country: "All of us from this day forth have but one task: to strike with all our might to preserve American freedom."

The attack on Pearl Harbor did more than just propel the United States into a war it had tried to avoid. In the most forceful way it served notice that America was vulnerable to attack. With the development of modern technology, especially the combat airplane, it would be difficult for any nation to feel safe from the scourge of war. The world was too small for that now, and while the world had been getting smaller, America's territory and foreign interests had grown. While the full meaning of this probably did not immediately become clear to all Americans, there was an immediate and almost total end to talk about isolationism. The country was at war, and assured of the rightness of their cause, the public gave uncompromising support to the government as it set out to win.

Young men by the thousands appeared at recruiting stations to volunteer for the armed services. As young able-bodied men donned uniforms to build a fighting machine that would eventually number twelve million, they were replaced in the labor force by women, teenagers, and senior citizens who proved themselves fully capable of doing everything from driving taxis to running steel mills. Women also entered military service as the armed forces sought to take full advantage of potential human resources.

Almost overnight the problem of unemployment disappeared. Industries greatly expanded their production by building new plants and operating 24 hours per day. From the assembly lines that had previously poured forth passenger cars, refrigerators, and radios, there now came a stream of tanks, guns, and airplanes. People learned how to "make do" with the old family car and how to patch up old appliances to keep them running. In spite of greatly increased earnings, in the interests of victory people learned to do without many things they had previously taken for granted. A large part of their savings went into the purchase of government war bonds to help finance the war which would add $220 billion to the federal debt, ten times the amount spent on World War I. This was total war, and there was a role for every citizen from the youngest to the oldest in what had become a global contest.

Americans learned a lot about geography from the war. Newspapers were read as never before, and the headlines daily carried news about far-off places with unfamiliar and strange sounding names. Often the headlines were accompanied by news maps showing the locations of these places and illustrating their strategic importance. Most Americans had relatives in the armed forces. At work, at home, at school, people had very personal reasons for talking more and more about what was going on in places like Casablanca, Iwo Jima, Anzio, and Normandy, and less and less about events in Omaha, Des Moines, Boston, and Pasadena.

While Americans on the home front were getting more familiar with the world via the news, millions of men and women in uniform were getting a firsthand acquaintance with Asia, Africa, and Europe. People who, without the war, would probably never have traveled beyond the borders of the United States, came into direct contact with others whose language, customs, religions, and attitudes were different. As the strange became familiar, it became increasingly difficult for Americans to view the world from the narrow prewar perspective.

One of the best signs that the United States was abandoning isolationism was the role this country played in the development of the United Nations. The United States played a leading role in all of the conferences and negotiations that led eventually to the San Francisco Conference of 1945. On April 25 of that year, delegations representing 50 nations met in San Francisco to complete the drafting of the United Nations Charter and bring the new organization into being. The United States was represented by a distinguished delegation including congressmen from both the Republican and Democratic parties.

By the time the conference had completed its work, the war in Europe was over. Harry S Truman, who had succeeded to the presidency when Roosevelt died in April, traveled to San Francisco to address the final session of the assembly. The new relationship of the United States to the rest of the world was made clear as the leader of the world's strongest power spoke to the delegates of 50 nations:

> We all have to recognize — no matter how great our strength — that we must deny ourselves the license to do always as we please. No one nation, no regional group, can or should expect any special privilege which harms any other nation. If any nation would keep security for itself, it must be ready and willing to share security with all. That is the price which each nation will have to pay for world peace. Unless we are all willing to pay that price, no organization for world peace can accomplish its purpose.
>
> And what a reasonable price that is!
>
> Out of this conflict have come powerful military nations, now fully trained and equipped for war. But they have no right to dominate the world. It is rather the duty of these powerful nations to assume the responsibility for leadership toward a world of peace. That is why we have here resolved that power and strength shall be used not to wage war, but to keep the world at peace, and free from the fear of war.
>
> By their own example the strong nations of the world should lead the way to international justice. The principle of justice is the foundation stone of this Charter. That principle is the guiding spirit by which it must be carried out — not by words alone but by continued concrete acts of good will.

Table 2–1 U.S. CASUALTIES IN MAJOR WARS	
Spanish-American War	4,108
World War I	320,518
World War II	1,076,245
Korean War	157,530
War in Southeast Asia	416,773
Total	**1,975,174**

Source: U.S. Department of Commerce

Table 2–2 U.S. PUBLIC DEBT		
Year	Total Debt	Share Per Capita
1974	$475,060,000,000	$2,241.92
1971	403,742,000,000	1,949.30
1955	274,374,000,000	1,660.11
1939	40,440,000,000	308.98
1920	24,299,000,000	288.23
1900	1,263,000,000	16.60

Source: U.S. Department of the Treasury

There is a time for making plans—and there is a time for action. The time for action is now. Let us, therefore, each in his own nation and according to its own way, seek immediate approval of this Charter—and make it a living thing.

Truman expressed his confidence that "the overwhelming sentiment of the people of my country" would mean speedy ratification by the Senate. He was right. After only six days of debate, the charter was ratified by an overwhelming vote, and the United States became a member of the United Nations.

The defeat of Japan was now only weeks away. On August 6, 1945, a single bomb exploded over Hiroshima, Japan. With a force equivalent to 20,000 tons of TNT, the first atomic bomb to be used in war did as much damage as would have been done by about one thousand airplanes releasing conventional bombs. In spite of this, the Japanese government refused to surrender. Three days later, another atomic bomb destroyed Nagasaki. On September 2, aboard the USS *Missouri*, the Japanese signed an unconditional surrender. World War II became history. Now came the more difficult job of building the peace.

What do each of the four statistical tables (2–1, –2, –3, and –4) tell you about the United States in the twentieth century? Find evidence in the tables to support or contradict the following conclusions:

1. As the United States produces more and more for itself, it depends less and less on foreigners.
2. During the past half century the United States has become both "richer" and "poorer."
3. In foreign trade, the United States generally gets the short end of the deal.
4. War is the main cause of the growing American public debt.

Table 2–3 U.S. GROSS NATIONAL PRODUCT

Year	Total Production
1972	$1,155,200,000,000
1970	977,100,000,000
1951	328,404,000,000
1945	211,945,000,000
1938	84,670,000,000
1933	55,601,000,000

Source: Bureau of Economic Analysis, Social and Economic Statistics Administration

Table 2–4 U.S. EXPORTS AND IMPORTS

Year	Exports	Imports
1972	$48,968,000,000	$55,282,000,000
1963	23,104,000,000	17,072,000,000
1958	17,755,000,000	13,298,000,000
1953	15,661,000,000	10,915,000,000
1948	12,545,000,000	7,183,000,000
1938	3,064,000,000	2,180,000,000

Source: U.S. Bureau of International Commerce

★ THE LEGACY OF WORLD WAR II

War sometimes makes strange bedfellows. For the sake of defeating the Axis powers, the United States and its allies found it convenient to unite with the Communist dictatorship in Russia in spite of the fact that the war was typically thought of as a campaign to preserve democracy. During the war, more military assistance from the United States went to Russia than to any other ally except Britain. Joseph Stalin, the powerful dictator of the Soviet Union, was affectionately pictured in the United States as "Uncle Joe." He played a leading role in all of the major conferences to determine the Allied strategy for victory. He committed the Soviet Union to agreements for the temporary division and occupation of the defeated countries when the war ended, and he pledged his country to cooperation through the United Nations and other means to help maintain the peace.

When the war ended, the spirit of cooperation quickly broke down. A long and dangerous "Cold War" began between the "Communist East" and the "Capitalist West." The Western democracies saw the Russians and their Communist allies as exploiters of the postwar problems who were determined to use any means possible to expand communism and destroy democracy. For their part, the Russians saw the West, under American leadership, as determined to keep Russia isolated and weak and prevent the growth of communism as an alternative to Western-style democracy.

In the postwar decades, the Cold War frequently turned hot. Fears of Communist expansion were greatly increased as Communist regimes rose to power in Eastern Europe supported by the Russian armies that had occupied those countries in the final phase of the war. In 1949, after a four-year civil war, mainland China came under control of the Communists led by Mao Tse-tung. The world's largest country, Russia, and the world's most populous country, China, joined in the Sino-Soviet pact. The following year, an army supported by the Communists invaded South Korea from North Korea. The United Nations responded, and in three years of fighting the Communist forces were pushed back into the north. Thirty-seven thousand Americans died in the conflict. At the same time, Communist revolutionaries were active in Southeast Asia where the stage was being set for another conflict even more costly to American life, the Vietnam War.

The Cold War was heightened by another important develop-

The Brandenburg Gate stands just inside East Berlin. Berlin, a divided city in East Germany, became a major symbol of the Cold War. What do you think is the significance of the Brandenburg Gate to the West German people? To East Germans?

ment arising out of the war. By the end of World War II, millions of people who lived in European colonies in Africa and Asia were determined to break away from European domination and establish their own independence. The United States, which had to make decisions about the fate of its own overseas empire, also had to decide what position to take on these nationalist movements in the colonies of its European allies. Russia, with no ties to Western Europe, was free to support the nationalist movements and to encourage regional "wars of liberation" in which local Communists sometimes played a leadership role.

Throughout the postwar decades the military and economic power of the Soviet Union continued to grow at a rapid rate, and a second "superpower" soon took its position as the rival of the United States. The "black and white" issues of communism *vs.* capitalism and dictatorship *vs.* democracy soon gave way to a much more complicated international situation.

In the aftermath of World War II, the United States found itself faced with a number of critical questions. Among them were the following:

1. World War II brought widespread devastation to large areas of Europe and Asia at the same time that it brought prosperity to the United States. What responsibility, if any, did the world's richest nation have for the reconstruction of the war-torn countries?

2. The war had left the United States in possession of the strongest military establishment in the world's history, including a monopoly on atomic power. Should the United States disband its military establishment or continue to support it as insurance against future wars?

3. Within the space of a quarter century, the United States had been drawn into two world wars. In the effort to preserve the peace, could the United States return to a "go it alone" policy, or should it enter into some form of "collective security" involving alliances and military commitments to other nations?

4. After World War II, millions of people in Africa and Asia were demanding their own right to be free of colonial rule and govern themselves. Should the United States risk antagonizing its Western European allies by supporting the freedom of Afro-Asians? What should be the fate of America's own overseas possessions?

5. During the campaign against the Axis powers, espionage and other tactics involving secrecy played an important role in victory. Should these same tactics continue to play an important part in Cold War strategy, or are espionage and secrecy incompatible with the traditions of a free and open society?

In the narrowest sense, these questions were issues of the period immediately following World War II. But, as we shall see, these basic issues took on larger dimensions as the war faded into the background. These basic questions are still alive today in a somewhat broader form. Together they make up the core of controversy around which Americans continue to debate the responsibilities of the United States to its neighbors on planet Earth.

In the following chapters, we will examine each of these issues. We will examine them not only in terms of their narrow postwar context, but also in terms of world realities today. As you examine the issues and alternatives open to the United States, your task will be to arrive at some conclusions of your own about the proper role of the United States in world affairs.

RICH NATION IN A
POOR WORLD—FOREIGN AID

The end of World War II brought great rejoicing in America. Across the land bells tolled, factory whistles blew, horns honked, and people flocked into the streets dancing and celebrating. Churches and synagogues were packed with worshippers giving thanks to God. Others found different ways of giving thanks as restaurants and nightclubs did a landslide business.

In other parts of the world where the battles had been waged, there might have been even greater cause for celebrating. But for many there was no joy. In large areas of Europe, North Africa, Asia, and the Pacific Islands, the rubble of war scarred the landscape. Great cities with their factories, shops, homes, schools, hospitals, and churches lay in ruins. The debris of numberless battles on land and in the air was strewn across the countryside. Great bridges, their backs broken, lay rusting in the middle of rivers. The roads they connected had been pockmarked with bomb craters and torn by the treads of tanks as they rumbled on to battle. Harbors were clogged with the twisted and torn wreckage of ships sunk by aerial bombardment. Millions of displaced refugees of all ages roamed aimlessly in search of families, homes, food, and jobs. The human losses were staggering. An estimated six million Jews had been systematically exterminated in Nazi concentration camps. Russia alone counted at least twenty million dead. The total number of deaths from the war would probably never be known.

As in the First World War, the United States escaped the full brunt of the holocaust. Americans went to the war before it came to them; the battles were fought on foreign soil. At home the full productive capacity of American farms and factories, enormously expanded by the war effort, remained intact. The federal debt rose to the astronomical figure of $247 billion as a result of the war. But Americans individually enjoyed unheard of prosperity. Wartime conditions of full employment, high wages, and overtime pay left people with fat savings accounts. After a short period of readjustment to a peacetime economy, these savings provided the basis for a period of economic growth unlike any in the history of the nation. For the sake of the war, people had gotten by without new cars, appliances, and other needs. Now they were in a spending mood. Wartime and postwar marriages produced a "baby boom" that helped to assure a growing demand for goods and services throughout the fifties and sixties.

It was against this backdrop of prosperity that the United States began its program of peacetime foreign aid—a program which has been a matter of controversy both at home and abroad ever since World War II.

Foreign aid is a catch-all term that includes many different kinds of assistance to other nations. There are two main categories: (1) *Military assistance* is aid which will help a country wage war or protect itself if attacked. (2) *Economic assistance* is designed to help a country overcome such basic problems as hunger, disease, inadequate housing, unemployment, and inflation. Military assistance is normally channeled through the Department of Defense. Most economic assistance is provided through the Agency for International Development (AID), which operates within the Department of State.

Aid is provided in a variety of ways. A direct grant or gift of money, food, equipment, or supplies may be donated to a country in need. But it has been more common in recent years to give loans or credits instead of grants. With a loan, the country can purchase the goods or services needed and then repay the loan at low interest over a long period of time. Often it is required that the goods and services be purchased in the United States. *Technical assistance* may be given by sending engineers, agricultural experts, or military advisers to a foreign country. Technical assistance may also be provided by bringing foreigners to the United States for education or training.

A U.S. adviser in Guatemala demonstrates how to use the tractor. What type of aid program does this photograph illustrate?

Some aid programs are *bilateral,* meaning that the United States agrees to provide direct assistance to one other country. Much of American aid, however, is channeled through *multilateral* arrangements with organizations representing many nations. Examples of multilateral aid are the assistance provided to the United Nations and such related organizations as the World Bank and the International Monetary Fund.

Obviously, foreign aid is a very complicated matter. Fortunately, it is not necessary to understand all the details about foreign aid in order to consider the issues involved. It is these issues with which we will be primarily concerned in this chapter: Should we provide aid to other nations? What kinds of aid should we give? What can we expect foreign aid to accomplish? Does the United States provide enough assistance to other countries? Does the United States provide too much? What is the future of foreign aid?

The following activity will help you to focus on the issues before we begin to examine the record of foreign aid.

Americans hold many opinions about the responsibility of the United States to give assistance to foreign nations. Below is a list of possible positions one might take on foreign aid. In your notebook, or on a separate sheet of paper list the numbers 1 through 8. For each corresponding statement listed below, write "A" if you agree, "D" if you disagree, and "U" if you are undecided. Save your list until you finish the chapter. Then repeat the exercise without looking at your original list. Compare the two lists to see whether your opinions have changed as a result of what you have read.

1. The United States should not give any aid to other countries.
2. The United States should only give aid to friendly countries.
3. Aid should be given to allies in time of war, but not to any country in time of peace.
4. Aid should be restricted to countries that are democratic. No aid should go to dictatorships.
5. The United States should give foreign aid only after it has taken care of all its needy people at home.
6. The United States should give military assistance to friendly nations for their own defense.
7. The United States should provide needy countries with economic assistance, but should never give military assistance.
8. The United States should only give the kind of economic assistance that will help another country overcome its problems and become more self-sufficient.

★ THE BEGINNING OF FOREIGN AID

Several months before the attack on Pearl Harbor, the Congress authorized the president to lease or lend any war materiel or supplies to any country whose defense was considered vital to American security. Under this "Lend-Lease Program" more than $40 billion in aid went to allies of the United States between 1941 and 1945. As soon as the war ended, however, it appeared that the United States was losing no time in getting out of the foreign aid business. On August 30, 1945, three days before the official Japanese surrender, Harry S Truman announced the end of Lend-Lease. However, temporary programs for the relief of war victims continued.

Pressure for more American aid grew during the following winter. Millions faced hunger and starvation as severe droughts ruined crops in some of the world's major food-producing areas, adding to the already serious food shortages. Compared to the average American diet of 3,400 calories, it was estimated that 104 million Europeans would be on a diet of less than 2,000 calories that winter. At this level, there would be a marked decrease in the ability of people to work and a high risk of disease.

Former President Herbert Hoover was appointed by Truman to head a Famine Emergency Committee to coordinate efforts to meet the crisis. Hoover traveled to Europe to make a personal investigation of conditions. His report from Poland in March 1946 indicated how bad conditions were. In Poland alone he found an estimated 1,100,000 war orphans. The capital city had been without bread for three weeks. From 50 to 70 percent of various types of livestock had been lost in the war, and dairy products were practically unknown to Polish children.

Estimating that there were 500 million people in Europe, the Far East, and India in need of aid, Hoover said: "I have never regarded starvation as a matter of race or creed." He appealed to his fellow Americans to voluntarily reduce bread consumption by 25 percent "in order that millions may survive who are otherwise doomed to death by starvation." It was in response to these kinds of immediate postwar needs that the United States, by the end of 1946, provided a total of $2.67 billion for relief.

It was widely believed that World War II was brought about by the failure of nations to deal effectively with the problems created by World War I. According to this theory, unsettled economic conditions—widespread unemployment, rapid inflation, high taxation, bankrupt governments—helped to set the stage for the rise of dictators like Mussolini and Hitler. Many leaders felt that, unless they did a better job of coping with problems created by World War II, new dictators might rise to power.

Out of frustration with the inability of their governments to help them, people might again turn to radical movements. Weak governments, unable to defend themselves, might easily fall victim to takeover by revolutionaries or foreign aggressors. According to this way of thinking, World War II could be the stage setting for World War III. Considerations such as these played an important part in making foreign aid one of the main instruments of American foreign policy. By 1970 the United States had invested about $128 billion in military and economic aid, and almost 100 countries had benefited in one way or another from American assistance.

★ EVOLUTION OF FOREIGN AID

The Truman Doctrine of 1947 marked the transition from temporary postwar relief to major programs of long-term assistance. In March of that year Truman made an appeal to Congress for $400 million in aid to Greece and Turkey where the governments were in danger of overthrow by Communist-led guerillas. It was in this speech that the Truman Doctrine was stated.

The Truman Doctrine

> The very existence of the Greek state is today threatened by the terrorist activities of several thousand armed men, led by Communists, who defy the Government's authority at a number of points. . . . Meanwhile, the Greek Government is unable to cope with the situation. The Greek Army is small and poorly equipped. It needs supplies and equipment if it is to restore authority to the Government throughout Greek territory. . . .
> Greece's neighbor, Turkey, also deserves our attention.
> The future of Turkey as an independent and economically sound state is clearly no less important to the freedom-loving peoples of the world than the future of Greece. . . .
> One of the primary objectives of the foreign policy of the United States is the creation of conditions in which we and other nations will be able to work out a way of life free from coercion [outside force]. . . .
> The peoples of a number of countries of the world have recently had totalitarian regimes forced upon them against their will. . . .
> I believe that it must be the policy of the United States to support free peoples who are resisting attempted subjugation [conquest] by armed minorities or by outside pressures. . . .
> I therefore ask the Congress to provide authority for assistance to Greece and Turkey in the amount of $400,000,000 . . . .[1]

---

[1] U.S., Department of State, *Bulletin*, XVI, No. 409A (Supplement, May 4, 1947), pp. 829–832.

As part of the American aid program for Greece, wheat is loaded into bags. Would you endorse this type of foreign aid?

In foreign policy, the term *doctrine* is used for a major statement of policy, usually by a president. A doctrine states a basic principle, or set of principles, which will guide American action in foreign affairs.

Find the Truman Doctrine in the preceding selection from Truman's appeal to Congress. Look for a statement which not only applies to the situation at that time in Greece and Turkey, but would also apply to similar situations in other times or places. Restate the Truman Doctrine in your own words. Do you think the doctrine represents a new departure in American foreign policy, or does it describe what the United States had already done in World War II? World War I? The Spanish-American War? Explain your answers.

When President Truman asked Congress in 1947 for $400 million to aid Greece and Turkey, some members of Congress probably thought his request was extravagant. However, the aid provided to those two countries under the Truman Doctrine must later have seemed like small change compared to the $17 billion he requested over the next four years for aid to Europe under the Marshall Plan. Americans first heard of the plan when Secretary of State George C. Marshall, for whom the program was named, set forth the proposal in an address at Harvard University on June 5, 1947. In his speech Marshall called for a joint undertaking in which European countries would combine their resources and know-how with assistance from the United States to put the European economy back on its feet.

Communist, as well as non-Communist, nations were invited to participate in the program. At first there were signs that they might cooperate. The Russian foreign minister attended a preliminary meeting to discuss the conference of European states in which the specific goals and strategies were to be worked out. Czechoslovakia accepted an invitation to the conference and Poland seemed interested. But Russia, which controlled these "satellite" governments of Eastern Europe, refused to allow their participation. Whether it was intentional or not, the Marshall Plan became a major factor in the Cold War.

Sixteen Western European nations met in Paris from June to September 1947 and drew up the cooperative plan for European recovery. On November 10, Secretary Marshall appeared before a joint session of the Senate Foreign Relations Committee and the House Committee on Foreign Affairs to urge speedy action by the Congress. Marshall appealed to American self-interest as well as to humanitarian motives in stating the case for American aid to Europe.

The Marshall Plan

It would be well . . . to deal briefly with what the area encompassed by those 16 nations plus western Germany has meant to us and has meant to the world. This community before the war accounted for nearly one-half of the world's trade.

They owned nearly two-thirds of the world's shipping. Their industrial production in terms of the basic commodities of coal, steel, and chemicals was before the war slightly greater than that of the United States. Their economy was highly integrated, each part depending upon the efficient working of the others. . . .

I do not have to tell you that this foreign economic program of the United States seeks no special advantage and pursues no sinister purpose. It is a program of construction, production, and recovery. It menaces no one. It is designed specifically to bring to an end in the shortest possible time the dependence of these countries upon aid from the United States. We wish to see them self-supporting. . . .

There is convincing evidence that the peoples of Western Europe want to preserve their free society and the heritage we share with them. To make that choice conclusive they need our assistance. . . .

Whether we like it or not, we find ourselves, our Nation, in a world position of vast responsibility. We can act for our own good by acting for the world's good.[2]

The European Recovery Act was signed into law on April 3, 1948. Three years later, its goals having been met, the program was ended. In his memoirs, Harry S Truman cited the success of the program and gave the United States and himself a pat on the back:

The job of economic rehabilitation was successfully accomplished at far less cost than had been anticipated. I had told the congressional leaders that I thought seventeen billions of dollars over a four-year period would do the job of economic rehabilitation successfully. Thirteen billions did it.

The Marshall Plan will go down in history as one of America's greatest contributions to the peace of the world. I think the world now realizes that without the Marshall Plan it would have been difficult for Western Europe to remain free from the tyranny of Communism.[3]

---

[2] U.S., Congress, Senate, Committee on Foreign Relations, *A Decade of American Foreign Policy*, 81st Cong., 1950, pp. 1270–1271.

[3] Harry S Truman. *Memoirs by Harry S Truman*, Vol. 2: *Years of Trial and Hope* (Garden City, N.Y.: Doubleday & Co., Inc., 1956), p. 119.

Compare this view of things with a Soviet interpretation of America's role in postwar Europe. What are the basic points of difference in the interpretations of the American motives for giving aid? Are there any ways in which the Soviet view of American purpose might be reconciled with what Marshall told the Congress?

As a result of the Second World War, Germany and Japan were put out of action as competitors of the USA. The USA was the only capitalist country to come out of the war with strengthened economic and military positions. However, after the end of the war, the USA ran into great difficulties. In connection with the stopping of war orders there was a decline in industrial production. In 1945, in the USA as a whole, industrial production was reduced by approximately 15 per cent . . . . In connection with the sharp reduction of deliveries under Lend-Lease, exports fell to $9,800,000,000 in 1945 as compared with $14,400,000,000 in 1944. Unemployment increased. Speculation increased and inflation grew. . . .

With the purpose of maintaining the huge wartime profits, American monopolies tried to insure a high standard of production, which in its turn rested on the problems of a fight for new foreign markets, for supremacy in the world market for raw materials, and of the increase in export goods and capital.

In order to maintain high profits in the situation of a decline in the purchasing power of the people, American monopolies began to speed up the export of commodities in every possible way, making maximum use for this of the postwar situation in war-ravaged countries. . . . Imperialist circles in the USA looked for a way out of the mounting difficulties by further development of foreign policy expansion. . . .

In the postwar period the USA openly advanced its pretensions to "world leadership." Its course [was] aimed at the establishment of world supremacy of American monopolies and at the preparation of a war against the countries of the Socialist camp [Russia and its allies] . . . .[4]

---

[4] From *A Soviet View of the American Past,* An Annotated Translation of the Section on American History in the Great Soviet Encyclopedia (Glenview, Illinois: Scott, Foresman and Company, 1964). First Published by The State Historical Society of Wisconsin, 1960. Reprinted by permission of Scott, Foresman and Company.

Crocodile (Moscow), 1947

American Motor of the Latest Type

In a simple drawing, a cartoonist can deliver a message that most of us would have to put into words. The cartoon above appeared in the Soviet humor magazine, *Krokodil* (Crocodile). What do you think the Russian cartoonist is saying? Reexamine the preceding selection giving a Russian interpretation of America's role in postwar Europe. Find a sentence or phrase that you think might be substituted for the cartoonist's caption "American Motor of the Latest Type." Why do you think your sentence or phrase would fit?

The cartoon on page 45 is one American cartoonist's view on United States aid to Europe. How does this cartoonist's viewpoint compare with that of the Russian cartoonist? Which cartoon do you think is closer to the truth? Why?

1945

1953

1961

Rich Nation in a Poor World—Foreign Aid **45**

The Cold War overtones of foreign aid were implied in the name of the Mutual Security Agency, which was established in 1951 as the Marshall Plan was drawing to a conclusion. The new agency, primarily concerned with "security," was given broad control over economic and technical assistance as well as military aid. By this time the United States was involved in the Korean War and aid was being given to the French to put down the Communist-led revolution in Southeast Asia. In 1954, the Act was revised to make the distinction between economic and military aid that continues to this day with economic assistance under the control of the Department of State instead of the Department of Defense.

A major criticism of American assistance in the first few years after World War II was that Americans were too preoccupied with helping Europe while millions of more needy people in the so-called underdeveloped lands were neglected. In Europe the main problem was one of recovering from the war, but most of the nations of the "third world"—Afro-Asia and Latin America had always been poor. Many people in these areas—especially in Latin America—became convinced that Americans and Western Europeans were engaged in a conspiracy to keep the poor nations from becoming prosperous and from competing with the more developed nations.

The first serious attention to the needs of the "third world" came in President Truman's second inaugural address in January 1949 sometimes known as the "peace and freedom" speech. It was the fourth point in his address that particularly caught the attention of the underdeveloped nations: "We must embark on a bold new program for making the benefits of our scientific advances and industrial progress available for the improvement and growth of underdeveloped areas." What came to be known as the "Point Four" program was only the start of a long series of efforts to help poor nations develop.

One of the most ambitious undertakings of this kind was the Alliance for Progress, which President John F. Kennedy first outlined at a reception for Latin American diplomats on March 13, 1961. In the following excerpts from Kennedy's speech, what similarities and what differences can you find in the proposed Alliance for Progress and the earlier Marshall Plan?

Alliance for Progress

. . . I have called on all the people of the hemisphere to join in a new Alliance for Progress—*Alianza para Progreso*—a vast co-operative effort, unparalleled in magnitude and nobility of purpose, to satisfy the basic needs of the American people for homes, work and land, health and schools. . . .

. . . I propose that the American Republics begin on a vast new Ten-Year Plan for the Americas, a plan to transform the 1960's into an historic decade of democratic progress. . . .

Let me stress that only the most determined efforts of the American nations themselves can bring success to this effort. They, and they alone, can mobilize their resources, enlist the energies of their people, and modify their social patterns so that all, and not just a privileged few, share in the fruits of growth. If this effort is made, then outside assistance will give a vital impetus to progress; without it, no amount of help will advance the welfare of the people.

Thus, if the countries of Latin America are ready to do their part, and I am sure they are, then I believe the United States, for its part, should help provide resources of a scope and magnitude sufficient to make this bold development plan a success, just as we helped to provide against equal odds nearly, the resources adequate to help rebuild the economies of Western Europe. For only an effort of towering dimensions can insure fulfillment of our plan for a decade of progress.

Alianza was born the following August in a conference at Punta del Este, Uruguay. At this meeting most of the republics of Latin America joined with the United States in a vast undertaking to overcome centuries-old social, political, and economic problems.

Jerome Levinson and Juan de Onís, in a book entitled *The Alliance That Lost Its Way*, took a close look at Latin America as the "decade of progress" was drawing to a close. Comparing the situation of Latin America then to the goals established years earlier at the Punta del Este Conference, they arrived at some disappointing conclusions about the effectiveness of the Alliance.

The first main goal set forth by the Alliance charter was to achieve an economic growth rate of "not less than 2.5 percent per capita per year." They found that, while there was economic growth, it was mostly offset by population growth. Through most of the decade, the actual increase in GNP was only 1.5 percent. Another goal was to narrow the gap between the extremely rich and the very poor with a more even distribution of income. A survey taken in 1968 showed little change since the beginning of the decade when 42 percent of national income went to the richest 10 percent of the population, leaving only 14 to 21 percent for the poor, bottom half of the population.

In spite of some industrial growth, there was still widespread unemployment. Because of population growth, food production per person was estimated to be 10 percent *less* than it was at the end of World War II. In education, another major goal of the Alliance, there was an increase in the percentage of children in primary schools. Still, due to increased population, there were an estimated 27 million children not in school in 1967 — three-quarters of a million more than when the Alliance began. Construction of low-cost housing was greatly outstripped by the growth of city slums.

With all these shortcomings, Levinson and Onís still concluded that the Alliance had promoted "a new development consciousness." Although there was general disillusionment with the Alliance for Progress, Latin Americans were more committed to, and capable of, planning their economies to overcome their ancient problems.

---

1. Population growth in the United States has usually been considered one of the important factors that has contributed to the economic growth and prosperity. Considering the record of the Alliance for Progress, why do you think population growth has the opposite effect in Latin America?
2. According to projections by the United Nations, between 1970 and the year 2000 the population of northern America (United States and Canada) may grow from 225 million to 376 million. Unless trends change, Latin America's population during the same period would grow from 212 million to 673 million. What importance do these estimates have for the United States? For Latin America?

★ WHAT FUTURE FOR FOREIGN AID?

There are many difficulties in making judgments about the value or effectiveness of foreign aid. Since most countries receiving assistance from the United States are required to meet certain obligations, it is hard to decide at the completion of a program the extent to which it is really a result of foreign aid. All of the goals of the Marshall Plan were fulfilled, and at less cost to the American taxpayer than was originally expected. But would it have happened anyway, even without American aid? It should be kept in mind that Europeans had all the basic skills and know-how to rebuild their countries after the war, and over 90 percent of the capital that did the job was European capital, not American. Yet, maybe it would not have happened without the initiative and support received from the United States.

Under the Truman Doctrine the United States gave aid to Greece to prevent that country from being taken over by the Communists. The country remained non-Communist and became a firm ally of the United States. However, some of the military aid provided by the United States was used in a military takeover of the government of Greece. The military regime ruled without elections for seven years, censoring its press, jailing its opponents without trial, and forcing many of its citizens into exile in other countries. There seemed to be little doubt that aid to Greece had resulted in a victory against the Communists, but had it been a victory for democracy and freedom?

The "negative" impact of large-scale assistance, which is not included in the plans, must be taken into account when foreign aid programs are being judged. The introduction of advanced agricultural techniques and modern farm machinery may bring an impressive increase in food production to a backward country. But farmers who do not receive, or do not accept, the new machinery may soon find themselves unable to cope with the stiff competition from their more "up-to-date" neighbors who benefited from American aid.

Another factor which should be taken into account in judging foreign aid is the impact on the United States itself. It has been estimated that over 80 percent of the aid given by the United States has been used to buy American goods and services. From this standpoint, the effect of foreign aid is to support American industry and provide jobs for American workers. Following this line of reasoning, some advocates of foreign aid say that we must take a greater interest in aid to the developing "third world" simply because we are going to depend more on them for raw materials and markets in years ahead.

In spite of these difficulties, the United States Congress each year is confronted with the question of the future of foreign aid. What happens to foreign aid each year depends largely on the perceptions of the members of Congress, and the people they represent, about what foreign aid has or has not accomplished in the past. In this, as in so many other things, what people think is true may be more important than what the truth really is.

W. Averell Harriman, a veteran diplomat and adviser to presidents, recalled how he faced the problem of misconceptions about the purpose of foreign aid back in the 1940s.[5]

> In the Marshall Plan days I used to have arguments in the congressional committees before whom I appeared when we were attempting to get those enormous appropriations. One time several congressmen were pressing me for indications that the Europeans were grateful. I told them that I thought gratitude was the last emotion that we wanted to evoke. In the first place, it's an emotion that doesn't last for long. It's the old story of the way to make an enemy is to lend a man some money. What we tried to do was to build respect and confidence. The congressmen pressed me rather hard, and I grew rather annoyed. Finally, I said something along these lines: "I know exactly what you would like me to do. You would like to have me bring pictures of children dancing in the squares of the provincial towns of France, waving American flags and singing 'God Bless America.'" I said, "That's exactly what I am *not* going to do. You can fire me if you want, but as long as I am here, that's exactly what we are not going to encourage. If it happens spontaneously, occasionally, why that is something else."

Many years later, Harriman was still appearing before congressional committees to encourage American assistance to foreign countries. In 1970 he testified:[6]

> . . . there are important reasons why we must continue our assistance to the developing nations. First of all is our moral obligation. We have been endowed with resources which have made it possible for us to achieve a prosperity unheard of in history, and surely we have an obligation to give a helping hand to the less fortunate.
>
> Secondly, our own economic life can be strengthened and expanded as other nations develop. Expanding trade and markets will add greatly to our own continuing prosperity.

---

[5]   From *America and Russia in a Changing World* by W. Averell Harriman. Copyright © 1970, 1971 by W. Averell Harriman. Reprinted by permission of Doubleday & Co., Inc.

[6]   From *America and Russia in a Changing World* by W. Averell Harriman. Copyright © 1970, 1971 by W. Averell Harriman. Reprinted by permission of Doubleday & Co., Inc.

Lastly, the very survival of our civilization is at stake. . . . 34% of the population of the world in the developed nations has 87½% of the world's gross national product, whereas the 66% in the less developed nations have only 12½%. It is not conceivable that a few countries can live indefinitely as islands of luxury in a sea of poverty.

Table 3–1 PER CAPITA GNP:
SELECTED COUNTRIES, 1971

United States	$5,073	Nigeria	$120
Sweden	4,690	Sudan	117
Canada	4,279	Zaire	114
Kuwait	4,170	Tanzania	103
Switzerland	4,158	India	100
Denmark	3,612	Afghanistan	90
Australia	3,370	Ethiopia	79
Luxembourg	3,331	Pakistan	79
Iceland	2,898	Burma	69
Spain	1,154	Indonesia	69

Source: U.S. Agency for International Development.

Table 3–2 DISTRIBUTION OF U.S. ECONOMIC AID, 1948–1972

Region	Population (Millions)	Aid Received (Millions)	Per Capita GNP (Regional Average)
Europe	326	$15,239.0	$2,785
Near East and South Asia	849	12,007.1	449 (N. East) 94 (S. Asia)
East Asia	417	8,089.2	725
Latin America	252	5,926.3	555
Africa	271	2,724.8	214

Source: U.S. Agency for International Development. Population figures for the regions were compiled by the author based on 1971 estimates. *Only* the countries actually receiving aid from the U.S. between 1948 and 1972 are included in the population estimates.

Examine Table 3–1. The ten countries listed on the left are among those countries with the highest per capita GNP in the world. The ten on the right are among those countries with the lowest. What did Averell Harriman say in his 1970 testimony to a congressional committee that is illustrated in this table? What responsibility, if any, do you think the richer countries have to the poorer?

Table 3–2 shows the total economic assistance given by the United States to various areas of the world between 1948 and 1971. The table also shows the approximate population of the area and the average per capita GNP for the region. Examine the table carefully, and do the following.

1. Write down any relationship you can find between the economic need of an area and the amount of aid received.
2. List as many reasons as you can think of that might explain any discrepancies you find between the amount of aid received by an area and the degree to which it appeared to be in need.
3. Rearrange the quantities of aid to the regions in terms of what you think the priorities should be.

If Harriman found it difficult in the Marshall Plan days to sell foreign aid to members of Congress, he must have found it even more difficult in 1970 when congressional support for foreign aid was rapidly deteriorating. In both 1971 and 1972 major appropriation bills for aid were defeated. The powerful chairman of the Senate Foreign Relations Committee, J. W. Fulbright, spoke of foreign aid as a "Cold War relic." In September 1972 during a debate over an amendment to an aid bill, Fulbright asked what had happened to all the great hopes and dreams of the bright future that foreign aid was supposed to bring about. He declared: "The reality of foreign aid is that all of these hopes, all of these dreams have gone aglimmering, and no amount of money can alter the situation or breathe new life into the corpse of foreign aid."

In January 1974 the House of Representatives voted by a whopping margin (248 to 155) *not* to contribute to the International Development Association (IDA). A branch of the World Bank, IDA was established with American help to provide long-term, low interest, loans for development projects in countries judged by the United Nations to be most needy. When IDA was established, the United States pledged to provide $1.5 billion (spread over four years) of the $4.5 billion to be contributed by 25 sponsoring nations.

Robert McNamara, president of the World Bank, called the congressional action an "unmitigated disaster for hundreds of millions of people in the poorest nations of the world." McNamara claimed that, in terms of aid for economic development, the United States now ranked 14th among the 16 principal donor countries. According to McNamara, the per capita income of Americans was 30 to 40 times that of people in the poor Afro-Asian countries helped by IDA. Yet, in relation to national income, Americans were only providing one-tenth as much aid to other countries for development as they had 25 years earlier.

The Nixon administration was stunned by the defeat of the bill, as were the 24 other donor countries. However, the debate over the bill revealed a number of reasons why congressional action was turning against foreign aid. Claiming that the United States couldn't afford a number of domestic programs, President Nixon had impounded (refused to spend) billions of dollars that Congress had appropriated for education, pollution control, highway construction, medical research, and combating poverty. One representative who voted against the bill complained "he was trying to get us to give Asians and Africans what he has denied to Americans."

Stanley Karnow, in *The New Republic* (February 9, 1974), described the congressional "Flight from Aid" and quoted several congressmen who gave various reasons for the opposition to funding IDA:

REP. TIM LEE CARTER (Kentucky): "Shouldn't we take care of our poor people first?"

REP. JOHN DENT (Pennsylvania): "Giving this aid to these countries without some kind of string attached puts us in the position of being suckers."

REP. JOHN FLYNT (Georgia): Described the bill as one of "those things which would be nice to have if we had the money to pay for them."

REP. WAYNE HAYS (Ohio): "Now some of the members can go home if they want to . . . and tell their constituents they voted for this $1.5 billion and at the same time tell them this money goes to these same countries that caused the price of gasoline to go up to 50 cents a gallon, the price of fuel oil to go up 100 percent. The Republicans can just keep voting like that and talking like that . . . and we Democrats probably will take more seats in the House than any party since this Republic was founded."

REP. GEORGE MAHON (Texas): "I am not going to vote to increase our commitments at a time when we cannot take care of folks at home, when the dollar has been under heavy pressure, when the national debt has increased by about one-fifth in the last four years, and when we are going into debt this year another $15 billion."

If you were a representative voting on the appropriation for the International Development Association, would you have joined the 248 who voted against the funds or the 155 who voted for them? In the following selection, you might try to imagine yourself as a representative and make your own judgment about the future of foreign aid. Incidentally, the Sahel region you will be reading about was one of the areas most dependent on the International Development Association for assistance.

★ WHAT WOULD YOU DO?

One of the most pressing problems of the world today is how to provide food for a population that is growing at an estimated 200,000 people *per day*, enough to populate a city of moderate size. While population has been growing, the world's food surpluses have been declining. In some areas prolonged periods of drought have been brought about by changing weather patterns and have brought the threat of starvation to millions. One of the most critical areas of drought has been the Sahel region, a band of territory that stretches across Africa on the southern rim of the Sahara. The 22,000,000 people of the Sahel depend primarily on agriculture and raising livestock. But years with little or no rain have pushed the sparse grasslands back and replaced them with desert sand, in some places by as much as 100 miles.

In "Death Stalks the Thirsty Sahel," Claire Sterling describes "a calamity of ghastly dimensions." As you read her account of conditions in the Sahel, determine what your own response would be if you were president of the United States.

> Along the southern rim of the Sahara, following its contours from the Atlantic to the Nile, an immense tract of land known as the Sahel is today suffering a calamity of biblical dimensions. Intensely hot and eternally parched for rain, the Sahel was never much good at sustaining life; now, after five terrible years of drought, about one hundred thousand people and some 20 million head of livestock have already starved to death, and the end is not in sight.
>
> Everywhere the Sahel's thin blanket of coarse grass and thorny bush is giving way to sterile sand. Live, moving dunes—killers of every growing thing—are forming even on the very banks of rivers, and for mile after mile nothing is left to show where the great Sahara ends and the Sahel begins. The six countries hardest-hit—Mauritania, Senegal, Mali, Upper Volta, Niger and Chad—are slowly slipping out of human use.
>
> **Shifting Sands.** Lying roughly between the 14th and 18th parallels above the equator, in normal times the Sahel, in its

southernmost parts, rarely gets as much as 23 inches of rain a year (mostly between June and October). This tapers off to almost none near the Sahara. The 22 million people of this devastated region divide into two segments: three quarters live south of the 14-inch rainfall areas, farmers who sow millet and sorghum at the start of the rainy season and reap these crops after its close; to the north where only hardy tamarisk and acacia trees, savannah grass and thorny bush can survive in temperatures that sometimes reach 122 degrees, nomadic herders of camels, sheep, goats, cattle and donkeys are all endlessly on the move for forage and water. In a centuries-old pattern, each year they head north during the rainy season; then, in the dry season, by agreement with the farmers, they start south, where their herds eat the stubble of harvested fields and drop fertilizing manure. At best, it is a precarious existence.

Beginning in 1968, the summer rains began to fail. For four years the southern farms got less than half the usual rain; the rangelands above, almost none. The desperate nomads began to move their herds southward indiscriminately, competing for the greenery left. Crops were planted and replanted, only to wilt under sand showers. Food supplies dwindled, and the governments, too poor to buy emergency supplies, hoped for more rain—in vain. By the time they launched an international appeal for help in 1973, it was tragically late.

The statistics are too unreliable to tell precisely how great is the human toll and how much land has already turned to desert. Mauritania, most severely afflicted of the Sahelian states, has had practically no harvest for two years now, except in the Senegal River Valley. "We are a nation on the dole," a regional governor sadly admits. "Four of every five persons are ruined." Chad reports that half its enormous territory is smothering in sand. And ecologists speak of areas where the desert is advancing serveral miles each year. The Sahel is heading straight for a complete breakdown. Some observers believe that after one more year of drought it could be finished forever.

In the Wasteland. I spent six weeks in the West African Sahel last autumn. Wherever I went, from the west coast of Mauritania and Senegal inland to Mali, Upper Volta and Niger, disaster was evident. After the first day I stopped counting the animal skeletons strewn by the wayside, the dead and dying trees bowed in haunting arches over acres of empty bush. In Niamey, the capital of Niger, I met proud

Tuareg tribesmen who had walked 700 miles from Timbuktu in search of food, burying one relative after another on the way.

Dozens of villages I passed were abandoned. In still inhabited settlements, farmers told me of having to eat all their millet seed before they could plant it. Nomad refugee tents, often mere straw-covered lean-tos, cluster around these villages, their inhabitants mostly women and children, the menfolk lost with the last of the cattle they tried to save. Their herds were the nomads' meat and milk, pack-animals, hides for their tents and wool for their clothes, bride-price and legacy for their children. Up to 90 percent of these herds are gone.

When I got to northern Mali, the military government had banned foreign relief workers and visitors from the refugee

The skulls of long-dead cows are the only remains of what was once a pasture of grazing cattle. What might be done to help the Sahelian people? How would you react to some of the suggestions in this article?

camps. But I was told of children living alone in squalor and one tent where seven youngsters squatted for days next to the body of their mother, waiting for her to "wake up." The misery I saw outside the camps was unnerving enough. In Gao, apathetic nomads sat in the sand-blown streets with their heads on their knees, too weak even to put out a hand for charity. And I will never forget a child of three I saw in the small hospital there who was shrunken to the size of a newborn infant. "He'll die tonight," the nursing sister said as she moved on to the next cot. "It's the ones with a chance that we must save."

In response to the human suffering, donor states last year rushed in 625,000 tons of grain (the United States contributed 256,000). But moving shipments inland where grain was most needed proved unspeakably difficult. Mauritania has fewer than 100 miles of paved road in its 411,000 square miles, while only Mali and Upper Volta of the Sahel's landlocked states have rail outlets to the sea. Tens of thousands of Sahelians died walking toward relief. More would have perished if an international airlift had not been organized to drop food where starvation was only days or hours away. Pilots of Hercules planes were especially gallant, making landings on pocket-size strips.

The tragedy is far from over. Last summer's rains were, almost uniformly, even less than those of the four previous years. Estimates of how much more emergency grain is needed to tide the Sahel over until next October's harvest—if it comes—run close to a million tons. By mid-March, 700,000 tons of that grain had been committed.

Deadly Delusions. The man was rare, among the hundreds I talked with in the Sahel, who saw anything but blind destiny behind the dreadful scourge visited upon the region. Yet, the worst of this tragedy is the blindness of man himself. Sahelians are not aware of making any mistakes. Indeed, in a land where periodic droughts have been common for centuries, their frugality is exemplary. I saw women walk for miles under a scorching sun to collect little prickly balls of cram-cram, a kind of wild grain. I saw millet planted in tiny plots of topsoil fenced in with straw matting to ward off the sand—the wilting shoots watered, one cupped handful at a time, by men walking back and forth from a shallow pool.

All the same, these people are mismanaging their precarious resources. One time-honored way of squandering them is to set bush fires every dry season to flush out edible desert rats, with a resulting impoverishment of the topsoil. Another is to lop acacia branches to round out a herd's diet, or chop down trees for firewood. Yet acacia forms the best canopy to break the winds, its leaves make rich humus and its roots stretch ten yards in all directions to bind the soil and trap rainwater. Deprived of the humidity these trees exude, the air gets drier, less able to attract rainbearing clouds, and the loosened topsoil is whipped away in blinding sandstorms. The denuded earth becomes iron-hard, unworkable for people with primitive tools, impermeable to the rains when they do fall.

Ironically, beneath the pervasive sand both the Sahara and the Sahel are awash in water. Huge ground-water basins lie 1000 feet and more below most of the region. At the request of Sahel governments, who think that more water is the desert cure-all, various foreign-aid programs, including those from the United States, have for years been tapping these deposits with mechanical rigs. Today the Sahel is criss-crossed with thousands of boreholes. Water from the deeper ones gushes up in such abundance that 10,000 head of cattle can drink their fill at a time from one. Yet nothing has done more than these boreholes to hasten the massive advance of the world's biggest desert.

Carried away by the promise of unlimited water, nomads forgot about the Sahel's all-too-limited forage. Centuries-old tribal agreements that apportioned just so many cattle to graze just so long in just so many locales were brushed aside. Enormously increasing herds, converging upon the new bore-holes from hundreds of miles away, so ravaged the surrounding land by trampling and overgrazing that each borehole quickly became the center of its own little desert 20 to 40 miles square. And once they had drunk all they liked, the cattle could no longer make it back to any remaining pasture. They died, not of thirst, but of hunger.

The Way Out. At their drought conference last September, the six most sorely affected West African states staked out their financial needs for recovery—about a billion dollars, double what they are getting now. Aside from grain purchases, the shopping list includes $200 million for water-development projects, of which a sizable chunk will go toward *more* boreholes; millions for replenishing herds, which not one of these countries seriously proposes to control; and only $26 million for reforestation, barely enough to stabilize 50,000 acres. Yet the desert *could* be forced back and the toll of future droughts minimized if sensible use were made of the money now about to flow into the Sahel.

Granted, the stricken countries need food and public-health assistance. But, most of all, they need a plan of range management, tree and forage planting and water control, plus the political daring to implement it. With proper controls, the Sahel could raise enough beef on the hoof to feed half of hungry Africa.

Actually, the most ingenious and efficient way to make the best of these lands was worked out by the nomads' own ancestors. If they would return to their old, delicately balanced grazing practices and combine them with modern range practices there would be a real payoff. The nomads would keep on the move with the seasons, as always, but their herds would be much smaller, better fed and cared for. Water, whether in wells or boreholes, would be spaced out to service only cattle allowed to graze in the vicinity. Trees would be replanted in the millions.

It is true that only courageous politicians would try to make the nomads limit their herds; yet they must be persuaded if they are to survive. And if the donor nations don't want to subsidize the Sahel for the rest of this century, they, too, must exercise foresight. Money should be tied to specific aims, such as reforestation. And *no* funds should be allocated for additional boreholes on the range unless largescale planting of forage and controlled grazing are part of the project.

When asked, the nomads invariably agree that their old way of life is finished. "Just give us something else to do and we'll do it," a wonderfully vibrant Tuareg widow told me over ritual glasses of mint tea in her Niamey refugee tent. Whether they get the chance will depend on the spunk of their governments and the insistence of their foreign friends.[7]

Examine each of the following statements. Which of the actions would you take? Which do you think would be unwise? Why?

1. Send all available surplus food in the United States to the countries of the Sahel.

---

[7] From "Death Stalks the Thirsty Sahel" by Claire Sterling. Reprinted with permission from the June 1974 *Reader's Digest.* Copyright 1974 by the Reader's Digest Assn., Inc. Condensed from *The Atlantic Monthly.*

2. Offer to provide airplanes, ships, and trucks to transport food and medicine donated by other countries to the Sahel.
3. Provide low interest loans to the governments in the Sahel region for purchasing food and supplies in foreign markets.
4. Send medical teams and agricultural specialists to the drought-stricken areas.
5. Set up population control clinics in the region to teach people to limit the size of their families.
6. Invite people of the Sahel to migrate to the United States and provide them with unoccupied land in this country.
7. Send drilling teams into the Sahel to drill more wells.
8. Donate livestock to replace the herds which have perished in the drought.
9. Pay Sahelian herders to limit the size of their herds and replant the areas stripped of vegetation.
10. Do nothing and let nature take its course.

ARMS AND DISARMAMENT

Since the beginning of the Cold War era, the superpowers have tried to achieve security by being so well armed that no potential enemy would dare to attack. At the same time, they have also sought security through the negotiation of agreements on arms control or disarmament. In spite of more than fifty disarmament conferences involving the United States and the Soviet Union since 1946, the arms race continues. Various partial measures in arms control have been agreed upon. But in the mid-seventies it was still estimated that about seven percent of world GNP, roughly $200 billion, was being devoted to armaments and war. By far the biggest portion of this amount was being spent by the United States and the Soviet Union. In 1975 the United States defense budget alone was over $80 billion, more than any year since the close of World War II. At the same time, heavy purchases of arms by other countries, including the poorest, were sustaining a multi-million dollar international trade in weapons. Of all the countries exporting weapons, the United States was the leader in sales with Russia running a close second.

The following activity will help you to clarify your own views as we examine the complicated issues of arms and disarmament.

Below is a list of statements expressing various opinions that people might hold on the issues of arms and arms control. In your notebook, or on a separate sheet of paper, list the numbers 1 through 5. For each corresponding statement listed below, write "A" if you agree, "D" if you disagree, and "U" if you are undecided. Save your list until you finish this chapter. Then repeat the exercise without looking at your original list. Compare the two lists to see whether your opinions have changed as a result of what you have read.

1. Regardless of cost, the United States, compared to other nations, should always be "number one" in military strength.
2. The United States should set an example by cutting down its own stockpiles of weapons.
3. Defense spending should never exceed one-fourth of the entire federal budget.
4. The U.S. government should end all research leading to the development of new and more sophisticated weapons.
5. The United States should negotiate agreements with the Soviet Union and other major powers to control arms.

★ HIROSHIMA: AN END AND A BEGINNING

Just one month before the outbreak of World War II in Europe, Albert Einstein, the brilliant scientist who had fled to the United States from Nazi Germany, wrote to President Franklin D. Roosevelt. The letter advised the president that recent work in physics demonstrated the possibility of producing an extremely powerful bomb by setting off a nuclear chain reaction in a mass of uranium. The letter also indicated that German scientists were already engaged in research to produce such a weapon.

The nuclear arms race began three years later when the British, the Canadian, and the United States governments agreed to cooperate in the top secret "Manhattan Project." The project, lasting three years and costing $2 billion, was designed to develop an atomic bomb before the Axis powers did. Germany had already been defeated when the dramatic climax came on July 16, 1945, on a desert site near Alamogordo, New Mexico. The first mushroom-shaped cloud produced by a nuclear explosion rose eight miles over the desert. As the night was transformed into a brightness surpassing the light of day, the project research director, J. Robert Oppenheimer, recalled some lines from a sacred Hindu poem:

If the radiance of a thousand suns
Were to burst at once into the sky
That would be like the splendor of the Mighty One . . .
I am become Death,
The Shatterer of Worlds.

Three weeks later, the "radiance of a thousand suns" burst over Hiroshima.

During the months prior to the dropping of the first A-bomb, heavily populated Japanese cities suffered day and night raids by B-29 bombers, and people in the industrial city of Hiroshima expected to be attacked at any time. A single raid sometimes involved hundreds of planes and resulted in more than 100,000 casualties, mostly civilians. Thus when three lonely planes appeared in the sky above Hiroshima on the morning of August 6, 1945, it was assumed that they were just on a reconaissance mission, not a bombing raid. The air raid warning was given, but soon gave way to the sound of the "all clear." The unsuspecting citizens of Hiroshima went on about their daily business. A few minutes later, 75,000 of them were dead or dying, and their entire city lay in ruins.

One of the survivors was a Methodist minister, Reverend Kiyoshi Tanimoto, whose recollections of the disaster were recorded by John Hersey in his book, *Hiroshima*. Rev. Tanimoto was two miles away from the center of the explosion. Warned by the flash of light that cut across the sky, Tanimoto barely had time to flatten himself behind some rocks before the blast hit the area where he had been standing. At first he assumed that a single bomb must have fallen right near by, and he was bewildered by the sight that confronted him as he climbed a small mound nearby and looked out over the city. Mr. Hersey gave the following account of Mr. Tanimoto's recollections of the bombing.[1]

From the mound, Mr. Tanimoto saw an astonishing panorama. Not just a patch of Koi, as he had expected, but as much of Hiroshima as he could see through the clouded air was giving off a thick, dreadful miasma. Clumps of smoke, near and far, had begun to push up through the general dust.

---

[1]   From *Hiroshima* by John Hersey. Copyright 1946 and renewed 1974 by John Hersey. Reprinted by permission of Alfred A. Knopf, Inc. Originally appeared in *The New Yorker*.

He wondered how such extensive damage could have been dealt out of a silent sky; even a few planes, far up, would have been audible. Houses nearby were burning, and when huge drops of water the size of marbles began to fall, he half thought that they must be coming from the hoses of firemen fighting the blazes. (They were actually drops of condensed moisture falling from the turbulent tower of dust, heat, and fission fragments that had already risen miles into the sky above Hiroshima.) . . .

Mr. Tanimoto . . . thought of his wife and baby, his church, his home, his parishioners, all of them down in that awful murk. . . . he began to run in fear—toward the city. . . .

. . . He was the only person making his way into the city; he met hundreds and hundreds who were fleeing, and every one of them seemed to be hurt in some way. The eyebrows of some were burned off and skin hung from their faces and hands. Others, because of pain, held their arms up as if carrying something in both hands. Some were vomiting as they walked. Many were naked or in shreds of clothing. On some undressed bodies, the burns had made patterns—of undershirt straps and suspenders and, on the skin of some women (since white repelled the heat from the bomb and dark clothes absorbed it and conducted it to the skin), the shapes of flowers they had had on their kimonos. Many, although injured themselves, supported relatives who were worse off. Almost all had their heads bowed, looked straight ahead, were silent, and showed no expression whatever.

After crossing Koi Bridge and Kannon Bridge, having run the whole way, Mr. Tanimoto saw, as he approached the center, that all the houses had been crushed and many were afire. Here the trees were bare and their trunks were charred. He tried at several points to penetrate the ruins, but the flames always stopped him. Under many houses, people screamed for help, but no one helped; in general, survivors that day assisted only their relatives or immediate neighbors, for they could not comprehend or tolerate a wider circle of misery. The wounded limped past the screams, and Mr. Tanimoto ran past them. As a Christian he was filled with compassion for those who were trapped, and as a Japanese he was overwhelmed by the shame of being unhurt, and he prayed as he ran, "God help them and take them out of the fire."

After four years of vicious fighting against the Japanese, there were few Americans in 1945 who questioned, either strategically or morally, the decision to use the bomb on Japan. President Truman said "I regarded the bomb as a military weapon and never had any doubt that it should be used." Winston Churchill wrote: "The decision whether or not to use the atomic bomb was never an issue." Ronald Steel speculates on why this "non-issue" of 1945 became an issue later on.[2]

More than two decades after the scientific triumph that became a political nightmare, we are still trying to come to terms with the decision to use the bomb. Burdened as we are with the terrible legacy of Hiroshima—the shame, the responsibility, and the fear—that decision strikes us as one of the most momentous this nation has ever taken. . . .

If it was not an issue in 1945, it has become one today. Why? Perhaps because our consciences are nagged by the suspicion that the sacrifice of Hiroshima and Nagasaki may not have been necessary. Perhaps because we have become more skeptical about the rhetoric which nations use to justify the impersonal violence of war. Perhaps because we are no longer so callous about the slaughter of the innocent, whether at Hiroshima or in the villages of Vietnam. And perhaps because today, unlike 1945, we feel the hot breath of the atom upon our own necks and know that our fate hinges upon a decision similar to the one made, or assumed, by American policymakers in the last months of the war against Japan.

At the time it was tested, the bomb seemed like an extension of the weapons already in use—different in degree, but not in kind. Being a weapon of war, it was used as a weapon of war. Today we find it shocking that it was dropped without warning on unprotected civilians as a device of terror quite divorced from any military significance. And it is. But the indiscriminate slaughter of civilians did not begin at Hiroshima. It was launched at Guernica and in Ethiopia, and developed on a larger scale at Rotterdam, Leningrad, and Dresden. [All locations at which civilian targets were bombed by Nazi or Allied airplanes before and during World War II.] It was refined by the U.S. Air Force in the fire raids against Japanese cities where civilians were the primary target. In a single raid on Tokyo, 83,000 people were burned alive—a toll greater than that taken by either of the atomic bombs. Few, however, bothered to question such brutality, although

---

2 From *Imperialists and Other Heroes* by Ronald Steel. Copyright © 1965 by Ronald Steel. Reprinted by permission of Random House, Inc.

among the few was Secretary of War Henry Stimpson, who later told Robert Oppenheimer that "he found it appalling that there had been no protest over the air strikes we were conducting against Japan which led to such extraordinarily heavy lossess of life . . . He did think there was something wrong with a country where no one questioned that."

Belatedly, but in growing numbers, such questions are being asked by a new generation of Americans, who see the dropping of the bomb on Japan as a decision which weighs heavily on all of us who are its descendants.

Examine the photograph (above) showing Hiroshima after the atomic blast and think about Rev. Tanimoto's experiences as you consider the following questions:

1. Was Secretary of War Henry Stimpson right in thinking that "there was something wrong" with Americans for not questioning the wholesale bombing of civilian targets in Japan?
2. Under which of the following circumstances, if any, would you favor the use of atomic weapons by the United States?

a. When it would be likely to shorten a war and save the lives of thousands of American service personnel.
b. When the destruction could be confined to a strictly military target with little or no loss of civilian lives.
c. In response to an atomic attack on one of America's foreign allies or an American overseas military base.
d. In response to an atomic attack on the United States.
e. Whenever there was an important military goal to be achieved, and it was certain there would be no atomic response by the enemy.

3. As indicated by Robert Steel, some people regard the A-bomb as "an extension of the weapons" already used before Hiroshima— "different in degree, but not in kind." Would you agree? Why or why not?
4. More than 40,000 American service personnel lost their lives in America's longest war—the war in Vietnam. If the use of atomic weapons would have shortened that war and saved American lives, as some believed, should nuclear weapons have been used in Vietnam? Explain your reasoning.

The Hiroshima Peace Shrine located at the center of the atomic blast.

★ SECURITY THROUGH ARMS?

The United States won the race with the Axis powers for control of the atom, but the smoke had hardly cleared over Hiroshima before another nuclear race was underway. In 1949 the Russians detonated their first atomic bomb. Shortly afterward President Truman announced that he had approved a project to develop a "super bomb" with more than 1,000 times the power of the bombs used on Hiroshima and Nagasaki. On November 1, 1952, the first thermonuclear hydrogen bomb was tested in the Pacific. Within a year the Soviet Union matched the American accomplishment with the test of its own thermonuclear bomb. Thus the pattern of the *arms spiral* was set—each technical advance by one side spurred a drive by the other side to match or overtake the opponent.

However, having the most powerful bomb would be of no advantage without the means of delivering it to an enemy target. The race to develop and stockpile constantly more destructive bombs soon gave way to a more expensive race to develop sophisticated delivery systems (long range bombers and rockets) and complex anti-ballistic warning and defense systems.

Both sides attempted to achieve a *first strike capability*—the capacity in a single attack to virtually destroy the enemy's ability to make war. For several years now, strategists on both sides have generally considered that first strike capability is an impractical, perhaps impossible, goal. Both Russia and the United States are so well armed that a different concept of "deterrence" has developed which some people regard as a "balance of terror."

According to the current idea of deterrence, a nuclear power would be discouraged from making a nuclear attack on another country if that country, or its allies, possessed *second strike capability*. This means the ability of a country, even after a nuclear attack, to retaliate with a devastating nuclear assault on its enemy. In the jargon of the arms race, the capacity of both of the superpowers to carry out a second strike is called *mutually assured destruction* (MAD). Some prefer to call it "dead man's revenge." By whatever name, the capacity for massive retaliation is regarded by many supporters of heavy defense spending as the key to preventing nuclear holocaust and maintaining world peace. As one person put it:

> Nuclear deterrence thus functions as a psychological weapon. . . . Like the gold in Ft. Knox, nuclear warheads can

remain safely stashed away in their shelters so long as everyone believes in their existence and their usability.[3]

But nuclear weapons are not always "safely stashed away," and even when they are, some people question whether they are safe. A number of fictional books and motion pictures have been produced since 1945 to raise the question of a possible nuclear accident; but, what happened on Monday morning, January 17, 1966, was not fiction. On that morning, six miles above the coast of Spain a giant B-52 stratofortress bomber maneuvered into position just under the tail of a KC-135 jet fuel tanker. The fueling boom snaked out from the tanker and found its way into the fuel intake of the bomber. Hundreds of gallons of highly volatile jet fuel were pouring into the thirsty B-52 when one of the bomber's engines suddenly burst into flame. As the flames licked toward the fuel line, the pilot gave the order to release armaments and then commanded the crew to bail out. Some crew members managed to escape, others did not, before the two giant birds exploded and plummeted earthward in a trail of black smoke and chunks of flaming metal.

The double disaster was witnessed by fishermen at sea and citizens of the remote village of Palomares, located just below the crash. In spite of efforts by Spanish and American authorities to quickly seal off the area, news of the crash traveled fast and attracted a number of curious sightseers from the surrounding area, among them an architect named Roberto Puig. Christopher Morris writes about *The Day They Lost the H-Bomb*.[4]

Roberto Puig was curious. Everyone for miles around was talking apprehensively about the air disaster. And the more he listened, the more curious he became. So Señor Puig, the municipal architect of Mojacar, decided to drive to Palomares and have a look around.

He had no business commitments that morning. What could be more pleasant than to motor along the winding coastal road, and then stroll down to the sandy beach? The sun was shining, and the temperature, although it was only January, was in the mid-seventies.

---

3   Helen B. Shaffer. "Nuclear Balance of Terror: 25 Years after Alamogordo," *Editorial Research Reports*, July 1, 1970, p. 489.

4   Reprinted by permission of Coward, McCann & Geoghegan, Inc. From *The Day They Lost the H-Bomb* by Christopher Morris. Copyright © 1966 by Christopher Morris.

Señor Puig, stocky and balding, deeply inhaled the fresh salty air with its tang of seaweed. There were no Americans or Spanish police in sight but he could see dozens of tiny figures in the distance combing through the fields by Palomares.

He decided not to venture too near the village as he knew he would only be turned back. So he plodded along the beach and round the headland. About half a mile ahead was the outline of the old Moorish fort, perched on a tiny cliff by the dried-up Almanzora riverbed. . . .

He walked on slowly and as he neared the fort noticed several men talking earnestly together. The architect took a winding footpath up the cliffside and soon found himself less than 100 yards from the fort.

It was then that his gaze was attracted by a strange object embedded in the dark brown soil and which was glinting in the sunlight.

He had no idea what it might be and walked across to take a closer look. He saw the object must have ploughed into the bone-dry ground with considerable force as it made a largish, egg-shaped crater.

Señor Puig knelt down to peer inside. To his horror he realised he was face to face with a bomb.

Sweat glistened on his forehead and his first reaction was one of incredible surprise. His next reaction was one of fear. For all he knew the bomb could explode at any minute. . . .

In fact, what Señor Puig had found was only one of four 25 *megaton*[5] bombs that the B-52 released just before its final plunge. The bomb that Puig stumbled on was one of three that were located within eighteen hours after the crash. The fourth bomb played "hard to get." It was not until 80 days later that it was recovered from a depth of a half mile in the sea, five miles off the coast. The search for the missing bomb, involving 130 divers with a fleet of surface vessels and special purpose submarines, reportedly cost American taxpayers about $1 million per day.

Each of these bombs was 5,000 times more powerful than the A-bomb dropped on Hiroshima. Although there are no large cities in the area, if they had exploded it was estimated that a minimum of 50,000 people would have died directly from the blast. The earth would have been scorched in a circle 100 miles wide, and deadly radioactive fallout could have spread across North

---

[5]   One *megaton* is equivalent in explosive power to one million tons of TNT.

Africa and Europe. However, embarrassed Air Force authorities were quick to assure the public that there was no danger since hydrogen bombs are very difficult to detonate. In fact, the Air Force let it be known that this was the thirteenth aircraft accident involving nuclear weapons since 1958, and none of them had resulted in a nuclear explosion.

One of the bombs involved in this accident did split its casing and spilled a quantity of radioactive material over the ground. The contaminated dirt was loaded into 4,810 steel ribbed barrels, each weighing over 500 pounds, and shipped to the United States for burial in a special plot for atomic waste. Tests at sea indicated no sign of radioactive spillage there. To prevent the tourist trade along the Spanish coast from suffering, the U.S. ambassador purposely went swimming off the coast of Palomares to demonstrate that there was no danger.

Whether the danger at Palomares was real or not, the incident of the missing H-bomb served to focus world attention once again on the reality of thermonuclear weapons. It again raised the question of whether real security could be found through constant multiplication of unthinkable weapons of mass destruction and an endless search for new and faster ways of delivering them to targets behind an enemy's defenses.

★ SECURITY THROUGH ARMS CONTROL?

As long as there has been a nuclear arms race, there has been a movement to bring nuclear weapons under control. Among the first supporters of nuclear disarmament was a group of scientists who worked on the Manhattan Project to develop the bomb. Their *Bulletin of Atomic Scientists* is still published today and keeps the public informed about the dangers of the nuclear age.

The Manhattan Project left three countries—Britain, Canada, and the United States—with the knowledge of how to make atomic weapons, but only the United States actually possessed the atomic bomb. These three countries joined to sponsor the establishment of the United Nations Atomic Energy Commission (UNAEC). This commission was set up in 1946 to work out the means for abolishing nuclear weapons and bringing nuclear power under control. Within a year after the defeat of Japan, the American representative to UNAEC, Bernard Baruch, presented a proposal for disarmament. Under the Baruch Plan, the United States offered to dispose of its entire stock of nuclear weapons and to turn over all information on the production of atomic energy as soon as UNAEC worked out a system for controlling nuclear power.

Russia, distrustful of the West and already at work on development of its own bomb, rejected the American proposal and offered one of its own. Under the so-called Gromyko Plan, the United States would demonstrate "good faith" by destroying its stockpile of nuclear weapons. Then, said the Russians, in an atmosphere of trust it would be possible to work out an agreement for the permanent international control of nuclear power. Suspicious of Russia's real intentions, the United States rejected the Gromyko Plan. President Truman wrote to Baruch: "We should not under any circumstances throw away our gun until we are sure the rest of the world can't arm against us." With few exceptions, this same kind of distrust has prevented any effective measures for arms control since 1946. Some limited steps have been accomplished since the Cuban "missile crisis."

The crisis had its background in three years of stormy Cuban-American relations that began when Fidel Castro took over the government of Cuba by force in 1959 and overthrew the dictator, Fulgencio Batista, who had been supported by the American government. There is considerable disagreement over who was at fault, but the governments of Fidel Castro and Dwight D. Eisenhower were at odds almost from the start. When the Castro government began to nationalize (take over) American-owned oil refineries and other businesses, President Eisenhower decided to support efforts to overthrow Castro.

Under the direction of the Central Intelligence Agency (CIA), anti-Castro Cuban exiles who had fled to the United States were given secret training and equipment to prepare an invasion of their homeland.

It was the newly inaugurated president, John F. Kennedy, who gave final approval to the ill-fated "Bay of Pigs" invasion in the spring of 1961. The invasion was a disaster and Fidel Castro remained in power, more secure than ever. Having declared himself a Communist, Castro became more and more committed to the Soviet Union for economic and military aid.

In October 1962 the Kennedy administration learned from aerial reconnaissance photos taken by a spy plane that the Soviet Union was installing intermediate range missiles in Cuba. These missiles, launched from bases only about 100 miles from the Florida coast, would be capable of carrying nuclear warheads to almost any city in the eastern United States. When confronted with the evidence of these missile installations, the Russians at first denied their existence. Later they claimed that the missiles were intended only to prevent another invasion of Cuba from the United States.

A reconnaissance photo of missiles installed by the USSR in Cuba. Why was Kennedy adamant about the removal of Soviet missles from Cuba? Why would Khrushchev think the USSR gained the most from the missile crisis?

Many of Kennedy's advisers suggested either an air attack on Cuba, an invasion of the island, or both. Kennedy rejected their advice. He also rejected the advice of Adlai Stevenson, the American ambassador to the United Nations, who suggested a compromise. Stevenson suggested that the Russians would probably be willing to remove the missiles if the United States agreed to remove its own Jupiter missiles from Turkish bases just below the southern border of Russia. Kennedy decided to yield nothing to Russia. Instead he ordered a "naval quarantine" of Cuba and demanded that the Soviets halt shipment of further missiles and withdraw those already on the island.

The U.S. Navy moved into position, ready to intercept Russian ships that were already on their way to Cuba. The Strategic Air Command, missile emplacements, and all American military forces around the world were placed on alert.

As President Kennedy prepared to go on the air to announce his decision to the American people, a copy of his address was delivered to Premier Nikita Khrushchev in Moscow by the American ambassador. The speech announced in part:

It shall be the policy of this nation to regard any nuclear missile launched from Cuba against any nation in the Western Hemisphere as an attack by the Soviet Union on the United States, requiring a full retaliatory response on the Soviet Union.

The Soviet Union was also warned that any retaliatory action taken by them in any other part of the world would meet with appropriate action from the United States.

The copy of the address delivered to Premier Khrushchev was accompanied by a special letter from Kennedy in which the president said:

The one thing that has most concerned me . . . has been the possibility that your government would not correctly understand the will and determination of the United States in any given situation, since I have not assumed that you or any other sane man would, in this nuclear age, deliberately plunge the world into war which it is crystal clear no country could win and which could only result in catastrophic consequences to the whole world, including the aggressor.

With an estimated 25 Soviet ships and submarines en route to Cuba and a determined U.S. Navy standing in their path, no one knew what to expect. A world which had become rather complacent about nuclear weapons suddenly found itself standing on the brink of nuclear war. In Washington preparations were made for the swift removal of the government to secret underground headquarters in the event of a nuclear attack on the capital. People went on with their daily routines, but hasty preparations were belatedly made in schools, factories, hospitals and other institutions for the protection of civilians. People anxiously listened to radios and stayed close to their television screens hoping for an indication of a change in the situation.

Finally, after days of suspense, the White House received word that some of the Russian vessels had stopped at sea and others were returning toward Europe. Secretary of State Dean Rusk remarked, "We're eyeball to eyeball, and I think the other fellow just blinked." More days passed before an agreement was finally reached by which Khrushchev agreed to dismantle and remove the missiles and the United States government pledged that it would not invade Cuba.

From beginning to end, the dangerous Cuban missile crisis lasted only thirteen days. Yet those thirteen days seemed to have taught the superpowers more about the need to control

As nearly as we can translate, it says: "We are agreed in principle on preventing the spread of nuclear weapons; however. . . ." —from The Herblock Gallery *(Simon & Schuster, 1968)*

nuclear weapons than the thirteen years since Russia exploded its first A-bomb and entered the nuclear race with the United States. In the next few years, a number of steps were taken to reduce the danger of nuclear war.

A "hot line" was established to provide instantaneous and direct communication between Washington and Moscow in the event of a future crisis. Russia, Britain, and the United States signed a limited Nuclear Test Ban Treaty agreeing not to conduct nuclear tests in either the atmosphere or the sea. Another treaty, in effect, made outer space a nuclear-free zone, not to be used for launcing war. On July 1, 1968, sixty nations signed the Nuclear Non-Proliferation Treaty. By this treaty countries with nuclear arms agreed not to share them with nonnuclear powers; and those without nuclear weapons agreed not to acquire them by any means.

In spite of these promising developments, the arms race went on. The number of countries with nuclear weapons, or the capacity to produce them, continued to grow; and many of them made no commitment to the various agreements designed to control nuclear weapons. When India surprised the world in 1974 with the test of its first atomic bomb, it brought membership in the "nuclear club" up to six—including the United States, the Soviet Union, Great Britain, France, and the People's Republic of China (Communist China).

Ingenious new weapons were developed by the superpowers to increase their ability to penetrate each other's defenses and maintain the delicate balance of mutually assured destruction. Fixed inside their massive concrete silos undergound, huge intercontinental ballistic missiles (ICBM's) waited patiently for signals that everyone hoped would never come. Nuclear submarines silently roamed secret pathways through the seas loaded with nuclear-tipped rockets, while long-range heavy bombers carried thermonuclear bombs through other secret pathways in the sky. To increase the chances of penetration, long-range missiles were equipped with a number of warheads (MIRVS), each capable of being redirected to separate targets once the missile had been launched.

In the face of the constantly rising danger and the extreme costs of the arms race, the United States and the Soviet Union finally agreed once more on a major effort to bring the race under control. They began the first round of the Strategic Arms Limitation Talks (SALT I) on November 17, 1969. The goal of this first round of negotiations was to reach an agreement which would provide a strategic nuclear *parity* by which each country would be roughly equal to the other in its nuclear strength. The agreement would limit the size of the nuclear arms stockpiles and delivery systems that each side could have. Then, with the race under control, another round of talks (SALT II) would seek to reach an agreement by which each side would gradually cut back its arms stockpile in a "balanced reduction."

On the surface, this sounds fairly simple, but nuclear *parity* does not mean that each side would have identical numbers of similar weapons. In fact, it was very difficult for SALT negotiators to agree on exactly what parity does mean. Not only the quantity, but also the quality, of weapons had to be considered. Russia had more missile launchers than the United States, and their missiles had greater power or "throw weight." But American missiles were more accurate, and they were equipped with multiple warheads. It was estimated that one U.S. Minuteman

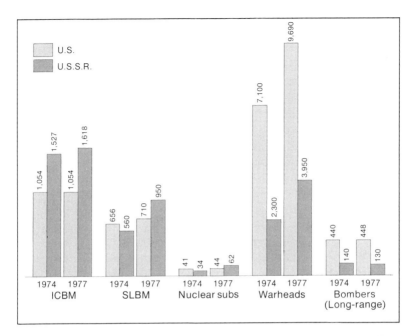

Figure 4-1. *Comparison of United States and Soviet Union nuclear strength.*

III with three warheads having a 600 *kiloton*[6] yield could do as much damage as three Russian SS-9 missiles, each carrying a 25 megaton warhead. There was also the size of the areas and the populations to be defended that had to be taken into account, as well as the comparative density of the populations concentrated in cities or spread through rural areas.

With all of these considerations and more, it took two and one half years of hard bargaining to reach agreement on parity. The SALT I agreement was finally signed in Moscow on May 26, 1972. SALT I placed specific limits on the number of strategic weapons each country could have by 1977. It was hoped that, by that time, SALT II would provide the means by which these quantities of weapons could be gradually reduced.

1. Examine Figure 4–1 (above) which compares United States and Soviet Union nuclear strength under the SALT I agreement. What examples can you find where an apparent advantage held by one

6   A *kiloton* is equivalent to one thousand tons of TNT.

side seems to be offset by a different advantage held by the other side? Do you agree that the limits set for 1977 represent a situation of parity?

2. Suppose that you were involved in the SALT I negotiations. Which of the following arguments would seem most reasonable to you if your real goal was to achieve a situation of parity? Discuss.

   a. RUSSIAN POSITION: "Our country is the largest on the earth — more than twice the size of the United States. We need more missiles for protection than you do."

   b. AMERICAN RESPONSE: "Your allies are right on the borders of your own country. The United States has committed itself to defending allies all around the world. Therefore, we need more missiles than you."

3. Pretend that you were a negotiator (either American or Russian) in the second round of SALT talks. Using the figures shown in Figure 4–1, what specific proposal do you think you might make that would help to reduce nuclear weapons, yet maintain security for both sides?

While SALT I was a significant step toward limiting the number of strategic weapons the superpowers could have, it did not bring the arms race to a halt. While limiting the number of missiles, the agreement did not place a limit on the number of warheads a missile could carry. It did not prevent either power from improving the quality of its weapons in terms of speed, accuracy, or the power to destroy. No restrictions were made on the smaller "tactical" nuclear weapons or nonnuclear conventional weapons. While the agreement limited the superpowers, it did nothing to control a global growth in armaments in other countries, many of which either have nuclear weapons or have the potential to develop them. Even after SALT I, defense budgets continued to grow.

★ HOW MUCH FOR DEFENSE?

Since the 1950s the defense budget of the United States has regularly consumed from one third to one half of all the taxes Americans pay. Supporters of defense spending claim that no cost is too high to pay for national security. Critics of defense spending, on the other hand, claim that Congress is really afraid to cut defense spending — that it has become a "sacred cow." Representative of these two viewpoints are the following statements by former Senator Margaret Chase Smith and Congressman Les Aspin.

MARGARET CHASE SMITH: *"It's Time to Speak Up for National Defense"*

For some time now, I have been growing increasingly concerned over a matter of public business which, it seems to me, ought to alarm all Americans. Yet, amazingly, I have heard little from my constituents or my Senate colleagues on the subject. Considering what is at stake — nothing less than America's ability to assure the future security and freedom of its people — the situation is incredible. Obviously, far too many Americans remain unaware of the frightful danger that is rising. As senior Republican member of the Senate Armed Services Committee, I feel I must speak out.

To put it as plainly as possible, there simply is no question that, if present trends continue, the Soviet Union will attain clear military superiority over the United States within the next few years. . . . Even now, in fact, the U.S.S.R. has far more land-based nuclear firepower than we have. It will equal or surpass us in submarine-based nuclear firepower by the middle of next year [1973]. It is embarked on an anti-submarine warfare program thay may eventually succeed in neutralizing much of our missile-carrying submarine fleet. It has an extensive ABM (anti-ballistic missile) development. It has been developing space weapons systems, as we have not. It has been modernizing and expanding its air and maritime forces, while we have allowed our own virtually to atrophy [waste away]. And the modernized Red Army may now well be at its best.

. . . Thus, today, our previously unchallengeable military supremacy is gone. And although we are in a state of rough strategic parity — equality — with the U.S.S.R., even that is eroding at a fast clip. In short, we are on the threshold of a world that will be unimaginably different from any that Americans have ever known — a world in which our President will not be able confidently to demand, for example, that the Kremlin remove its nuclear missiles from Cuba. Or that it refrain from constructing a missile submarine base on that island, or from establishing air bases there for its strategic bombers. Nor will the President be able to press credibly for equitable resolutions of problems at other points of vital interest, such as the Middle East or Berlin. Our President, whoever he is, will have to negotiate as best he can from a position of weakness — if he gets a chance to negotiate at all.

For, make no mistake, we are rapidly approaching a day

when the United States will be subject to all sorts of diplomatic blackmail and a strategy of terror waged by the Soviet Union. That is what the U.S.S.R.'s hugely expensive, decade-long military buildup is all about. There is no other logical reason for it. Moreover, as military ascendancy passes to the Soviet Union, the danger will increase that an over-confident Kremlin leadership will miscalculate, will try to impose its will somewhere in some way that will prove intolerable to the American people and will trigger nuclear war.

Unfortunately, this is not mere Pentagon propaganda, aimed at silencing opposition to defense spending and scaring Congress into apportioning a larger slice of the federal budget to the military. No one would be more delighted than I if we could safely eliminate military spending altogether and turn our full attention to improving the quality of American life — to refurbishing our cities, eradicating poverty, disease and crime, and solving our environmental problems. But first things must come first. As President Nixon has pointed out, if we are less strong than we should be, there soon may be no domestic society to look after.[7]

CONGRESSMAN LES ASPIN: *"To Much of a Necessary Thing"*

Surely national defense must always demand a large share of our attention, energies, and wealth. But there is the problem of "too much of a necessary thing." Bread may be the staff of life, but a diet of nothing but bread is bad for our health. We must have balance and proportion in our national priorities as well as in our diets. When our elderly citizens and poor school children go hungry; when our cities choke on polluted air; when our streams are too foul for swimming; when millions are unemployed — can we say that our national priorities are in balance? I think not . . .

Defense, we are all agreed, is a basic necessity. But the high priority we give to national defense demands a critical analysis of the level of defense spending compared to the resources devoted to other pressing needs.

The need for a critical review of defense spending has never been greater and the opportunities for defense budget cuts have never been better. With the cost of the Vietnam

[7] From "It's Time to Speak Up for National Defense" by Senator Margaret Chase Smith. The *Reader's Digest*, March 1972, pp. 66–67. Copyright 1972 by the Reader's Digest Assn., Inc. Reprinted by permission of Reader's Digest.

War winding down, and the conclusion of the SALT agreement with the Soviet Union, and the prospects of future international arms agreements, the resources devoted to national defense compared to other domestic priorities must be reexamined. The present political and diplomatic climate around the world gives us a unique opportunity to reduce the mammoth resources currently devoted to national defense.

Unfortunately, since the advent of the nuclear age and the Cold War, defense has become a sacred cow. Huge defense budgets are jealously protected by the military bureaucracy, their industrial allies, and a large number of Congressmen whose constituencies benefit from excessive defense spending. . . .

There was a time (in the late 1950s and early 1960s) when our federal budget suffered what economists call "fiscal drag." The federal government was actually collecting more money than was needed and the bureaucrats in Washington were constantly dreaming up new ways to use the extra funds. But now many Americans have recognized the need to expand our social services and clean up our environment as well as pay for national defense.

It is estimated, for instance, that the annual cost of comprehensive health care will require, at a minimum, an additional $35 billion of new federal revenues annually. President Nixon's proposed programs of revenue sharing for the cities and income maintenance for the poor are expected to cost $5.6 billion and $6 billion respectively each year. It is estimated by the President's Council on Environment Quality that the cost of cleaning up the environment will be $298 billion.

While some of these estimates may be exaggerated there is no doubt that the crunch is on. In the next few years it will be fiscally impossible to continue to accelerate defense spending and, at the same time, begin to attack . . . [these] problems. . . . In short, the federal government is going broke.

. . . The average American must begin to fight for a reordering of our national priorities. Otherwise future historians will look upon us as the nation that committed moral, physical, and spiritual suicide in the name of the sacred cow known as national defense.[8]

---

8 From *The Helpless Giant* by Andrew Hamilton with an introduction by Congressman Les Aspin. Copyright © 1972 by Schocken Books Inc. Reprinted by permission of Schocken Books Inc.

Table 4–1   U.S. DEFENSE BUDGET
For Selected Years, 1950–1974

Fiscal Year	Budget Requests	Appropriation
1950	$13,248,960,000	$12,949,562,000
1954	40,719,931,000	34,371,541,000
1959	38,196,947,000	39,602,827,000
1964	49,014,237,000	47,220,010,000
1969	77,074,000,000	71,869,828,000
1974	81,100,000,000	74,200,000,000

Source: U.S. Department of Defense, House
Appropriations Committee

Le Pelley in *The Christian Science Monitor* © TCSPS

'And we have to persuade everyone else not to carry one'

82   THE UNITED STATES IN WORLD AFFAIRS

"HOWDY, MIRV. IT'S NICE TO KNOW SOMEBODY ELSE IS WASTING MONEY."

Copyright © 1973 The Chicago Sun Times. Reproduced by Wil-Jo' Associates, Inc. and Bill Mauldin.

1. Examine Table 4–1 which shows the amounts of money requested by the president for the defense budget and the amounts actually appropriated by Congress. Do the figures tend to support or contradict Congressman Aspin's claim that the defense budget is a "sacred cow"?

2. Examine the two cartoons by LePelley (*Christian Science Monitor*) and Mauldin (*Chicago Sun-Times*). Do the cartoons represent essentially one point of view or two? What do you find in the cartoons to support your answer? Do either or both of the cartoons represent your own point of view? Explain.

One example of the on-going race between the Soviet Union and the United States for weapons superiority is a giant experimental aircraft the Russians have been testing over the Caspian Sea. Calling the aircraft the "Great Caspian Sea Monster," *Time* magazine gave the following description.

One awesome example of the Soviet Union's improving military technology is this gigantic vehicle. Now being tested over the Caspian Sea, the aircraft is the largest in the world, weighing an estimated 500 tons.

The Soviet design employs a revolutionary principle: the jet blast from the eight engines mounted on the stubby forward wing is aimed to hit the water and bounce back up under the main wing to create a lifting bubble of air similar to that on which Hovercraft ride. When fully developed in the late '70s, the creation is expected to thunder along at speeds up to 350 m.p.h. while flying only 25 to 50 feet above the water—low enough to make radar detection difficult. What is more, the huge aircraft could make two- to three-day voyages extending as far as 7,000 miles.

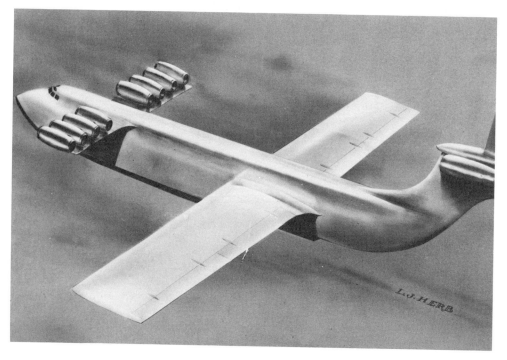

The "Great Caspian Sea Monster" is a Soviet experimental aircraft.

Loaded with gear and used for anti-submarine warfare, the monster would not make the American seaborne nuclear deterrent vulnerable overnight. But the strange aircraft would give the Russians a new and ominous means of hunting the U.S. Polaris/Poseidon and Trident submarines as they cruise in the silent depths of the seven seas.[9]

Suppose that you were a representative faced with a request by the Department of Defense to spend one billion dollars in developing an American version of the "Great Caspian Sea Monster." How would you react to each of the following statements by a spokesperson for the Department of Defense? Would you approve the request?

1. "Deterrence can only work if the United States remains at least as strong as the Soviet Union. The new Russian aircraft will destroy the delicate balance of power that keeps the peace unless the United States has a similar weapon."
2. "We can waste money by refusing to spend. If the United States allows Russia to gain the advantage this airplane could give them, our country will waste the billions it has already spent on nuclear submarines armed with missiles."
3. "The development of such a weapon would, in the long run, be a good investment in civilian transportation. Civilian versions of this military aircraft could provide fast low cost transportation of civilians."

★ WHAT WOULD YOU DO?

In recent years a number of bills have been introduced in Congress to establish a "Department of Peace." However, such bills always seem to get "pigeonholed" or die in a committee without ever getting to the floors of Congress for open debate. In the following selection, David Krieger of the Center for the Study of Democratic Institutions explains why he thinks a Department of Peace is needed.

---

[9]   From the "Great Caspian Sea Monster," *Time* Magazine, February 11, 1974. Reprinted by permission from *TIME* The Weekly Newsmagazine; Copyright Time Inc.

We must recognize clearly . . . that national defense is no longer possible. There can be no illusions that our cities are protected by our impressive array of nuclear armaments. Strategic weapons do not protect; if we are lucky, and so far we have been, they deter. Because we have avoided nuclear war for over a quarter of a century is no guaranty that we can look forward to another quarter-century of deterrence. Even if we accept the premises of . . . deterrence, there always remains the possibility of mistake; the failure of "fail-safe."

We have one agency in our government that concerns itself with problems of weapons reductions. This is the Arms Control and Disarmament Agency [A.C.D.A.], which was established in 1961. The agency is charged with carrying out research, negotiating, providing public information, and, when appropriate, direction of U.S. participation in control systems. The director of the agency reports to the Secretary of State and to the President.

The major difficulties with this agency as a force for peace and security in the U.S. government are that it is understaffed, is provided with insufficient funds, and is too much subject to the influence of the military. The agency has only 170 employees and an annual budget of approximately ten million dollars. This compares rather unfavorably with the annual budget of the Department of Defense (D.O.D.) of eighty billion dollars and a D.O.D. research buget of nearly ten billion dollars. It seems logical to ask why we allocate so much for research on weapons which cannot under any circumstances defend us, and so little in comparison on studying approaches to weapons reduction. . . .

One may well wonder at the value priorities on a government which devotes eight thousand times more money for weapons incapable of providing protection than it spends on attempting to increase security through the development of strategies of weapons reductions. However, even were A.C.D.A. to be given a larger budget and expanded staff, it is still unlikely that it would effectively fulfill its function of developing adequate strategies for disarmament. Nor would it be likely to fulfill its function of informing the public of the serious need for disarmament and the degree of insecurity inherent in the current nuclear deterrent approach to national security. The agency would be inhibited in fulfilling these functions by the influence of former military and Defense Department officials serving in advisory capacities. (Six of the fifteen current members of the General Advisory Committee of the Agency are former members of either the military or D.O.D.) . . .

It would seem that the United States (and all other nations as well) could now use a new agency of government, a department devoted solely to the study and implementation of peaceful resolutions to international conflicts. This department would be responsible for advising the President and informing the public on the dangers of nuclear weaponry and the threats to national and individual security posed by a continuation of the policy of deterrence and continued expenditures for more sophisticated weapons systems. It would also be responsible for recommending alternative strategies to those proposed by the D.O.D. and the State Department. The concern of this department would be peaceful conflict resolution and its secretary would be expected to advocate policy positions based on this concern in the same way the State Department argues for the national interest and the D.O.D. argues for national security through armaments.

The new department could be called the Department of Peace and its chief administrator the Secretary of Peace. The secretary would sit on the President's cabinet and on the National Security Council. The department would serve as a symbol of the nation's commitment to peace, and an agency of government receptive to peace proposals. The department would be expected to stimulate peace research and education, coordinate with similar agencies in other governments, and inform the public and Congress concerning the reduction of security due to nuclear armaments and international conflict. The Secretary of Peace would serve as chief advocate of peace and the reduction of insecurity created by the strategy of nuclear deterrence.[10]

Pretend that a bill for a Department of Peace has found its way to the floor of the Senate where you, as a senator from your state, are about to speak on the proposal. Which, if any, of the following types of statements do you think you might include in your speech?

[10] From "We Need a Department of Peace" by David Krieger, *The Center Magazine*. Reprint from the November/December 1972 issue of *The Center Magazine*, a publication of the Center for the Study of Democratic Institutions, Santa Barbara, California.

1. Starting a Department of Peace to compete with the Department of Defense would be starting a new "Cold War"—this time, inside the United States government!
2. We can't afford a Department of Peace . . . but we can't afford a Department of Defense either. Let's stop wasting our money on defense and let our "enemies" waste their money instead of ours.
3. The Department of Defense is the best "Department of Peace" that money could buy. The proof is that, in spite of the arms race, we have lived for three decades in a nuclear world without having nuclear war.
4. The American spirit of democracy and free enterprise depends on choice and competition. Let's create a Department of Peace and get back into that "good old American spirit."

CONTAINMENT OR DETENTE?

Each year, on the anniversary of George Washinton's birthday, a traditional address is read in both houses of Congress. The speech was originally delivered by Washington on September 17, 1796, as he neared the end of his service as the nation's first president. The speech, usually referred to as the "farewell address," has always been a favorite of isolationists. At great length Washington advised his countrymen to "steer clear of permanent alliances with any portion of the foreign world," and said:

> The great rule of conduct for us in regard to foreign nations is, in extending our commercial relations, to have with them as little political connection as possible.

If President Washington could return today, certainly one of the things that would astonish him would be the degree to which his country has become politically and militarily entangled with other nations in various parts of the world.

United States policy in foreign affairs for a century and a half following Washington's presidency could be described as a "go it alone" policy. The United States departed from that principle temporarily in World War I and again in World War II. As the

Cold War developed, America again turned its back on Washington's advice. In opposition to communism, the United States entered into a number of alliances and assumed the role of "leader of the free world" with commitments to defend more than forty other nations around the globe. Since 1945, millions of American servicemen have served abroad on dozens of American military bases that form an arc around the Communist world.

In recent years, a number of developments have changed the international scene considerably. Although about one third of the world's people are still ruled by Communist regimes, communism is no longer a single unified movement. The two Communist giants, the Soviet Union and the People's Republic of China, have become opponents in a sharp competition over ideology and leadership. The so-called satellite countries of Eastern Europe, as well as Communist parties and regimes in other parts of the world, have demonstrated greater independence of Moscow. While there are still dangerous tensions, as illustrated by the arms race, the Soviet Union and the United States have been learning to get along and even to work together on matters of common interest. President Richard Nixon's historic trip to China in 1972 opened the door to friendly relations with that country after two decades of bitter hostility. Soon after President Gerald Ford came into office, diplomatic recognition was extended to East Germany, and the door seemed to be opening to normal relations with Communist Cuba.

Some people now question the wisdom of continuing America's far-flung commitments abroad, and a new spirit of *neo-isolationism* (new isolationism) is growing. While some are calling for a withdrawal from foreign commitments, others claim that the apparent relaxation of tensions is not necessarily permanent, and may even be deceptive. They believe that better relations can only be possible if the United States remains on guard around the world.

Before we set out to examine the issues of America's foreign commitments, use the following activity to sort out your own views on these questions of American involvement.

Below is a list of statements expressing various opinions that people might hold on the issues of America's foreign commitments. In your notebook, or on a separate piece of paper, list the numbers 1 through

7. For each corresponding statement listed below, write "A" if you agree, "D" if you disagree, and "U" if you are undecided. Save your list until you finish this chapter. Then repeat the exercise without looking at your original list.

Compare the two lists to see whether your opinions have changed as a result of what you have read.

1. The United States is so powerful economically and militarily that it should not give — or accept — help from anyone.
2. Weaker nations should receive the protection of the United States.
3. The United States should never ally itself with dictatorial governments just because they happen to be "anti-Communist."
4. Forming alliances with other countries is a device the United States should use to gain influence over the affairs of other nations.
5. Forming alliances with the United States is a means other countries should use to get economic and military aid from the United States.
6. Even when the United States is not involved in a war, this country should have large numbers of servicemen and women stationed overseas to protect United States interests.
7. The United States should never back down in the face of Communist expansion in any part of the world.

★ COLLECTIVE SECURITY

It must have been a terrifying experience to be a German soldier on the morning of June 6, 1944, standing on the coast of Normandy and looking out to sea. This was the long-awaited "D-day" and one of the largest invasions in the history of warfare was about to begin. As far as the eye could see, the surface of the English Channel was covered with allied ships approaching the shores of France. On that day, 176,000 allied troops under the command of General Dwight Eisenhower landed on the Normandy beaches to face a withering barrage of German bullets and artillery. Within weeks, over a million British, French, and American forces were pushing toward Germany. As these forces closed in from the West, the Russian army advanced from the East squeezing Germany like a nutcracker. Ten months after D-day, on May 8, 1945, the war in Europe was over. Another four months brought victory over Japan, and World War II passed into history.

With the war over, the United States began to demobilize its army. There were 3.5 million American troops in Europe at the end of the war. Four years later, more than 97 percent of them

Soviet Union Control in Europe

had been withdrawn. Russia, on the other hand, did not demobilize its army. Backed by Russian troops, Communist regimes loyal to Moscow came to power in a corridor of East European countries. Germany was divided, with East Germany under Russian occupation and West Germany occupied by the Western allies. With the end of the war, cooperation between Russia and the Western allies broke down. In the words of Winston Churchill, an "iron curtain was drawn across Europe."

A series of events in the late 1940s aroused the concern of the United States about the intentions of Russia and her Communist allies. In 1947 aid was provided to Greece and Turkey under the Truman Doctrine to combat Communist-backed efforts to overthrow the governments of those countries. Russia not only refused to participate in the Marshall Plan, but prohibited her East European satellites from working with their Western neighbors in European recovery after the war. Communist parties in West European countries, like France and Italy, propagandized against the Marshall Plan as an American imperialist scheme to control Europe. In 1948 the Russians blockaded the city of Berlin, which had been jointly occupied by the Allies but was located 100 miles inside the iron curtain. Through the winter of 1948–1949 an American airlift kept West Berlin supplied with thousands of tons of food, fuel, and clothing. In the spring, the Russians accepted defeat and reopened the roads to Berlin. In 1949 the Russians detonated their first atomic bomb. And in that same year, Communist forces in China under Mao Tse-tung took control of the Chinese mainland and allied themselves with Russia.

Faced with all of these developments, the Western powers, and especially the United States—came to the conclusion that a giant Communist conspiracy was underway to bring all of Eurasia, and eventually the world, under the domination of Moscow. In response to this challenge, the United States developed a counter-plan to contain the Communists within their borders. This *containment policy* involved a number of strategies including the use of foreign aid, the formation of anti-Communist defensive alliances, and the establishment of military bases around Communist borders.

The first main area of concern was Western Europe, and here the United States led the way in the development of the North Atlantic Treaty Organization (NATO) as a bulwark against Communism. NATO, like other alliances to follow, was organized on the principle of *collective security.* The original alliance included the United States, Canada, Great Britain, France, Iceland, Norway, Denmark, the Netherlands, Belgium, Luxemburg, Portugal, and Italy. Greece and Turkey became members in 1952, and West Germany was added in 1955 to make a total of fifteen members.

According to the principle of collective security, all of the members are pledged to come to the aid of any member which is attacked by a country outside the alliance. Knowing this, a potential aggressor would have to think twice about starting a war. Following the lead of the West, Russia joined with its East European allies in a similar arrangement known as the Warsaw Pact.

On the tenth anniversary of NATO, the U.S. State Department published a booklet describing the organization and reviewing its record of service to the Atlantic alliance. Claiming that "NATO has never been exclusively a military alliance," the booklet set forth the official argument for American participation in the pact. As you read the following statement, what political, economic, and cultural arguments can you find for American involvement in NATO?

The truth that our own national fate and that of Europe are indissolubly linked has been grimly impressed on the American people twice within the last generation. Having learned that the broad Atlantic no longer shelters us from the conflicts of the Old World but may be used instead by an aggressor as a path to our door, we have sought to assure our security by defensive alliances in many parts of the world.

As Secretary Dulles [secretary of state under President Eisenhower] has pointed out, "No single nation can be truly independent and the master of its own destiny if it stands alone against the massive menace of 900 million people and their military and economic resources, solidified by international communism into a monolithic, aggressive force dedicated to world domination."

U.S. adherence to the NATO alliance is a recognition that Europe's freedom and strength are vital to America's own safety. There can be little doubt that, if free Europe were to fall under Soviet control, the addition of its huge industrial manpower resources to those of the Soviet bloc would decidedly shift the balance of world power against the United States and the rest of the free world.

The reasons for this are manifold. Europe's 335 million people possess an intellectual and technological capacity of the highest order. After the United States, Western Europe's industrial plant is the most highly developed in the world, and our joint industrial capacity far outstrips that of the Soviet bloc. In an age when science is the key to military strength, free Europe's undisputed scientific prowess becomes a vital element of Western defense.

With over three million highly trained and well-equipped men under arms and millions more in reserve, Western Europe has both the means and the will to resist any aggression. The European area provides the West with strategically located ports and air bases from which, in the event of Soviet aggression, retaliation would be swift and sure.

The United States has an important stake in the continued freedom of Europe from Soviet domination. Western Europe is by far the largest customer for American goods. On the other hand, it helps supply the United States with many of the raw materials without which our military and civilian production would be severly handicapped.

But America's interest in the security and continued freedom of Europe is based on more than considerations of mutual economic benefit or a common need for collective defense. It has its roots in a shared history and civilization and a fundamental community of interest. To our European progenitors we owe the foundations of our religion, art, music, literature, social customs, economic practices, and democratic freedoms. Indeed it is in defense of these values of Western civilization that the Atlantic Community has banded together to seek peace and security.

It is for all these reasons that NATO is to be considered, as President Eisenhower has said, "a basic and indispensable element of American defense alliances against the continuing Soviet Communist threat to the peace and security of the world."[1]

---

1. Examine the statement by the U.S. State Department and select the passages which you think explain the political, economic, and cultural reasons for American participation in NATO.
2. Do you think these arguments for participation in NATO are as true today as they were in 1949 when NATO was formed or in 1959 when the State Department published this statement? Why or why not?

★ SPREAD OF CONTAINMENT

Even before the formation of NATO, the United States was involved in a defensive alliance with 20 Latin American republics. The Inter-American Treaty of Reciprocal Assistance (or Rio Treaty) was signed in 1947 and operates under the Organization of American States (OAS) to provide a common defense for the Western Hemisphere. In addition to these commitments, the United States entered into defense pacts with the Philippines, Japan, South Korea, and the Republic of China (Taiwan). The Southeast Asia Collective Defense Treaty (SEATO Treaty) was signed in 1954. SEATO included several of the countries mentioned above, but added Pakistan and Thailand to American commitments. Also, at least according to the American interpretation of the SEATO Treaty, the United States became responsible for the defense of South Vietnam.

As the United States traced the spread of the "Communist menace" eastward into China, Korea, and Southeast Asia, the

---

[1] U.S., Department of State, *NATO, The First Ten Years (1949–1959)*, Publication 6783, March 1959, *passim.*

Containment or Detente? **95**

policy of containment followed. Almost every new alliance meant the extension of American military aid to the countries involved. More often than not, it also meant the building of new American military bases. By the end of the 1960s, in addition to hundreds of thousands of American personnel serving in Europe and the Mediterranean, about one million United States military personnel were stationed along the rim of Asia. Inside this web of alliances and military bases, the Communist menace was supposedly contained.

However, the containment policy did not always prevent the Cold War from turning hot. It took more than paper alliances to stop the Communist expansion in Korea, where more than 40,000 American lives were lost between 1950 and 1953 to maintain the independence of South Korea. It was also during these years that the United States began to play a role in the French war against Communist revolutionaries in French Indochina. United States involvement in this conflict grew until the Americans found themselves bogged down in the longest, and perhaps the most controversial, war of their history—the Vietnam War.

Indochina (Vietnam, Cambodia, and Laos) was part of the French empire from the mid-nineteenth century to World War II, when the area was taken over by the Japanese. When the French tried to regain control of Vietnam after the war, they found a nationalist organization, the Viet Minh, prepared to fight for Vietnam's independence. The Viet Minh was dominated by the Communist party of Indochina under the leadership of Ho Chi Minh. Unable to settle their differences by negotiation, the French went to war against the Viet Minh in 1946, and fought unsuccessfully for eight years to hold onto their empire.

At first the United States took a neutral position on the French Indochina War. As the containment policy was extended to Asia, however, American policy changed to one of support for France. In 1950 under President Truman the United States began to provide military aid to the French, and by 1954 was providing about 80 percent of their total war costs. In spite of all this assistance, the French were defeated and withdrew from Indochina in 1954. According to an agreement worked out in Geneva, Cambodia and Laos were given their independence. Vietnam was "temporarily" divided at the 17th parallel (17° latitude) into North Vietnam, which was controlled by Ho Chi Minh, and South Vietnam, which came under the control of a non-Communist leader, Ngo Dinh Diem.

The Geneva Agreement provided for elections to be held in

1956 to reunite Vietnam under one government chosen by the people. But bad relations between North and South prevented the elections from ever being held. Ngo Dinh Diem, with strong backing by the United States, was determined not to let South Vietnam "fall to the Communists."

The Eisenhower Administration began to provide limited assistance to South Vietnam in 1954, paying most of the costs of operating the government. Several thousand military advisers were also provided to help train the South Vietnamese army to fight the Viet Cong—a Communist guerilla organization fighting in the South Vietnam countryside with support from North Vietnam.

Under President Kennedy, the American involvement was increased. More military advisers were sent, and they began to accompany South Vietnamese army units into combat areas. Military supplies were increased, including helicopters flown by American pilots which ferried South Vietnamese troops and supplies into the battle zones.

The American role was tremendously escalated under President Johnson to the point that American troops assumed the major burden of the fighting. Before the end of Johnson's term of office the United States had a half million troops in Vietnam,

"THANKS A LOT."

and American B-52 bombers had conducted the heaviest bombing raids in the history of aerial warfare over North Vietnam.

In his campaign for election in 1968, Richard Nixon claimed that he had a secret plan for ending the war in Vietnam. But after he came into office, it took four more years before the "secret plan" finally brought an end to the war. Gradually forces were withdrawn, and after a settlement was negotiated in Paris, all American troops were finally withdrawn from the country. In spite of the peace settlement in 1973, fighting continued in Vietnam and so did aid in the form of American military supplies and equipment upon which the South Vietnamese army depended.

During the Nixon years the war spilled over into Vietnam's neighbor, Cambodia, where the U.S. Air Force conducted heavy "secret" bombing raids. The Congress did not grant President Ford's request for additional aid to Cambodia and South Vietnam in April 1975. The fall of these two countries appeared inevitable.

During nine years of air warfare in Indochina, U.S. airplanes dropped about three times as many bombs (over 7 million tons) as they did in all of World War II. The air war cost an estimated $16 billion, resulted in the loss of more than 8,000 planes and helicopters, and cost the lives of over 4,200 airmen. Examine the cartoon by Wright (page 97). Which of the following do you think best expresses the message of the cartoon or would you suggest another "message"?

1. The USAF was destroying their land, but Southeast Asians still appreciated American assistance in the fight against communism.
2. Americans were so determined to win that they didn't care who got hurt in the process.
3. Southeast Asians just wanted the Americans to go away and leave them alone.
4. If people want to keep their freedom, they have to be willing to sacrifice.
5. Now that the war was over, the survivors could begin to rebuild their country in peace.

At the height of the Vietnam War it was estimated that the war was costing American taxpayers from 3 to 4 million dollars per *hour!* The length of the war, its immense costs, and the heavy toll of American lives were all among the reasons why the war was so strongly opposed by a large segment of the American public. But even beyond these reasons, there were many who questioned whether there was any legitmate reason for American participation. When the administration claimed that the war was being fought to save South Vietnam from being forcefully taken over by the Communists, anti-war critics claimed that the South Vietnamese regime was as bad, if not worse, than any Communist government. It was constantly charged that the South Vietnamese government was riddled with corruption and ruled through a dictatorial police state that was kept alive by American aid. Nguyen Cao Ky, who became premier of South Vietnam in 1965, on one occasion casually remarked to news reporters that one of the historical figures he most admired was Adolph Hitler.

In Vietnam, as well as in other places, where there was no long tradition of democracy and human rights, the United States frequently found itself saddled with an alliance that was embarassing, troublesome, and costly. William J. Lederer, in his book *Our Own Worst Enemy*,[2] recounted an experience he had in South Vietnam which gives some insight into the kinds of problems Americans faced in trying to work with the Vietnamese.

> My first experience with the Vietnamese black market occurred in Saigon. I told the Army public relations officer at JUSPAO (Joint United States Public Affairs Office) that I planned to go out with troops, and asked where I could buy jungle fatigues and jungle boots.
>
> "We have lots of goodies for reporters if they have the right papers," he said, handing me an authorization to buy Army uniforms.
>
> A friend took me, on the back of his scooter, to the big PX in Cholon, where the Army uniform shop is. Outside the compound, with its sandbags and U.S. armed guards, was a place for customers to park their vehicles. As the vehicles were parked, small Vietnamese boys ran up, their hands outstretched, demanding "watch-your-jeep [or scooter] money." They wanted money to stop "someone" from cutting ignition wires or letting air from tires. These miniature gangsters shook down American customers almost directly in front of the U.S. guards.

---

[2] From *Our Own Worst Enemy* by William J. Lederer. Reprinted by permission of W.W. Norton & Company, Inc. Copyright © 1968 by William J. Lederer.

I angrily told a PX officer about the situation. He replied, "The street is Vietnamese territory. We are guests in this country. We have no jurisdiction over anything that happens in the street. Those kids can sell stolen PX merchandise out there and we can't touch them. Only the Vietnamese police can do anything.

"There was a Vietnamese policeman standing twenty feet away . . ."

"I assure you there's nothing we can do. We are guests in this country . . . and that's the way General Westmoreland [Commander of U.S. forces] has ordered it."

I made the obvious remark that it was a strange way to treat guests who were dying by the thousands to protect their hosts.

The major shrugged and said, "This is their country. We are fighting and dying in combat *because we have permission from the Vietnamese to be on those battlefields.* Parking scooters on their streets is something else."

A sergeant entered. "Major, the old woman is selling soft drinks and cigarettes — it's all our merchandise — right in front of the PX entrance."

The major sighed wearily. He had to play the same phonograph record again. "Our hands are tied unless we catch her stealing the stuff from the PX. Forget about it." Then he asked the sergeant to take me to the uniform shop.

When I gave the clerk my authorization he shook his head. "We haven't had fatigues or jungle boots for months."

"When are you expecting them?"

He held up his hands and shrugged.

We returned to the street, mended the cut ignition wire on the scooter, and returned to JUSPAO. There I told the colonel that the store did not have jungle uniforms.

He laughed and said that I would have to find them where he and his men did — on the black market. "They may charge you a couple of bucks more, but the gear is always available and in all sizes. . . ."

I walked down the street past the USO and the flower markets and the sidewalk restaurants. It took about five minutes; and there was the "Tiny Black Market" (the name implying that there were bigger places elsewhere). . . .

I continued up and down the stalls looking for uniforms and jungle boots. There were none visible. Then one of the black market operators came up and, speaking in English, asked me what I wanted. When I told her, she said "All complete uniform. Everything. Helmet. Pants. Boots. Shirt. Everything. Forty-five hundred piasters or thirty dollars. You want?"

"Are they new?"

"New. You want?"

"I want to see them."

"You buy them if new and right size?"

"Yes."

The woman turned to a boy, spoke to him in Vietnamese and gave him a piece of paper, then turned to me.

"Go with boy."

"Do I pay you?"

"Pay when you get clothes."

The boy took me several blocks along the street of the hardware stores. After a while we entered a store that had copper pots in the window. The boy went to an old man who was clacking an abacus. Without speaking, the old man led me out the back of the store, across a yard, into an alley which stank of rotten vegetables, and then up two flights of dark stairs into the loft of another building.

The place looked like a U.S. Army ordnance ammunition depot. Everything seemed to be painted brown and to smell either of oil or fresh paint. Ordnance equipment was arranged in orderly lines, and neatly printed price tags hung from everything. Automatic rifles were $250. A 105-mm. mortar . . . was priced at $400. . . . There were about a thousand American rifles of different kinds standing neatly in racks. M-16's cost $80. On one side of the loft were uniforms of all services, including the U.S. Air Force. There was even U.S. Navy diving equipment.

The old man inquired as to my sizes, and brought me the uniform and boots. After I had tried them on, he said, "That will be thirty-five dollars in U.S. money."

I told him I had no U.S. money.

"Your personal check is okay."

"No, I have only piasters."

"Okay, okay," he grumbled, "five thousand piasters."

Later that evening I talked about the black market to an old friend whom I shall call Tran Trong Hoc . . . .

He said, "What you saw is nothing. Go down to the waterfront some day and see how the big operators work. The whole South Vietnamese government—from Ky down—is involved."

"Any Americans in on it?"

"Plenty are becoming millionaires—exactly as happened when the U.S. Army occupied Japan and Germany."

"How do you know?"

"The black market in Vietnam is about ten billion dollars a year—all in American goods and monies. This could not exist without American collusion. It would be impossible. For example, everyone in Saigon talks about how La Thanh Nghe of Ky's cabinet has gotten about a million dollars in kickbacks from American pharmaceutical firms. There has to be American collusion. You couldn't lose ten billion dollars a year without it."

I did not answer.

"We'll go to the waterfront in a few days," said Tran Trong Hoc, " and watch the big operations."

"Let's go now."

"We have to plan it well. I need a few days. If we are not careful, neither of us will be alive to tell what we saw."

Suppose that you were an American taxpayer during the years of the Vietnam War and you had just read William Lederer's report on the Vietnamese black market in your newspaper? How would you react?

1. I'd write a letter to my representative demanding an investigation of the black market in Vietnam.
2. I'd contact the White House and go on record as being opposed to the Vietnam War.
3. I'd refuse to pay my income tax until the United States got out of Vietnam.
4. I'd participate in an anti-war demonstration.
5. I'd assume that this was only one side of the story, and that the United States government knew what it was doing.
6. I'd shake my head and turn to the sports page or the comic strips.

Just as the United States was gradually drawn into the Vietnam War, American forces were gradually withdrawn under President Nixon's policy of "deescalation." Negotiations went on for years in Paris with the North Vietnamese while President Nixon insisted upon what he called a "peace with honor." Finally, an agreement was reached, and the last American troops left Vietnam in August 1973.

Unlike the ending of most wars, there was no great national celebration in the United States. In general, Americans just seemed to be relieved that the war, at least for them, was over.

For the Vietnamese, however, the war was far from over. The cease-fire agreement quickly broke down and fighting continued into the Spring of 1975. Thirty years of continuous battle finally came to a close on April 30, 1975. Following the unconditional surrender of the South Vietnamese government, the victorious Communist armies marched into the streets of Saigon.

Just one week before the collapse of South Vietnam, President Gerald Ford spoke to an audience at Tulane University in New Orleans:

> We are saddened, indeed, by events in Indochina. But these events, tragic as they are, portend neither the end of the war nor of America's leadership in the world. Some seem to feel that if we do not succeed in everything everywhere, then we have succeeded in nothing anywhere. I reject such polarized thinking. We can and should help others to help themselves. But the fate of responsible men and women everywhere, in the final decision, rests in their own hands. . . . I ask that we accept the responsibilities of leadership as a good neighbor to all peoples and the enemy of none.

Examine the map (page 104) showing the amount of territory controlled by the Communists in 1965 (before the big buildup of American forces) and in 1973 when American forces were withdrawn. Consider the following questions as you draw your own conclusions about the outcome of the Vietnam War. (Note: *contested areas* means territory which both sides claimed to control.)

1. Did collective security and the policy of containment work in Vietnam?
2. Did the United States achieve President Nixon's goal of "peace with honor"?
3. Should the United States have continued to fight in Vietnam?

★ WHAT WOULD YOU DO?

With the withdrawal of American troops from Southeast Asia, the focus of the overseas forces issue shifted to Europe. After three decades of peace, more than 300,000 United States forces still remained on guard in Europe. For a number of reasons, people began to ask why.

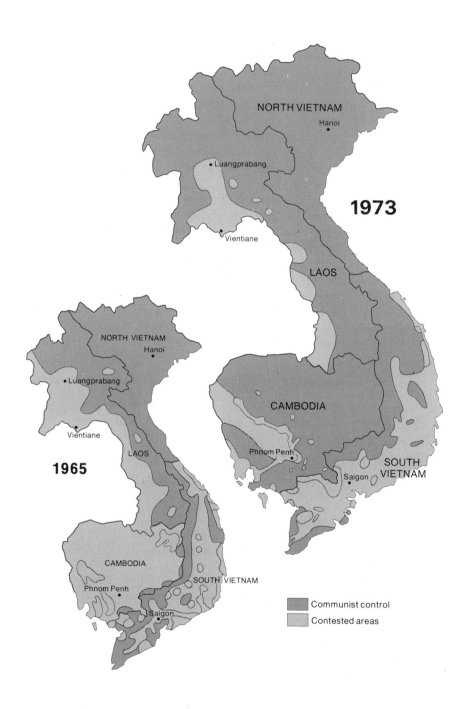

Communist Gains in Indochina

One of the main reasons was the great progress that had been made toward *détente* between the United States and the Soviet Union. *Détente* (pronounced day-tont) is a French word that refers to the relaxation of tension that comes when people get to know and understand each other. It does not mean an alliance, or even friendship. Under the leadership of Henry Kissinger, secretary of state for Presidents Nixon and Ford, *détente* has been one of the main goals of American foreign policy. In a news conference, Kissinger cautioned that we are not trying to reach *détente* with the Soviets because we have suddenly become friends. Rather, he said, we need *détente* because we are potential enemies—each having the power to destroy the other.

Progress toward relaxation of Soviet-American tensions actually began long before the Nixon administration began to speak of *détente*. As we have already seen, significant progress was made during the 1960s, while Nikita Khrushchev was Premier of the Soviet Union, in regard to matters of nuclear arms control. Khrushchev, who recognized the dangers of nuclear war, became a very controversial figure in Communist circles because of his constant emphasis on peaceful coexistence with the West. Some observers thought that his "too friendly" attitude toward the United States played a major part in his fall from power. But with the new Soviet leadership of Leonid Brezhnev the Nixon and Ford administrations continued to make progress toward good relations. A series of summit conferences of American and Soviet leaders resulted not only in successful negotiations on strategic arms limitation, but on a number of other vital matters as well.

The United States sold wheat to the Soviet Union when its own harvest was hurt by poor weather. Soviet-American trade has significantly expanded in both quantity and the number of items traded. There has been Russian-American cooperation in geographical exploration, medical research, and the exploration of outer space. Cultural exchanges involving thousands of artists, writers, dancers, and athletes have been a regular feature of Soviet-American relations. Every year thousands of American tourists board planes in New York destined for Moscow. There is even some limited investment by Western "capitalists" in the Communist Soviet economy, and some American banks have been permitted to open offices in Russia.

With all of this harmony and goodwill, people ask why hundreds of thousands of American military personnel are still on duty in Europe. Once again, the cry is raised to "bring the boys home." But, in spite of all the progress toward *détente*, the administration claims that potential dangers in Europe have not disappeared and troops are still needed. The following selections from an article in *U.S. News & World Report* set forth the major arguments that surround this controversy.

How much longer should the U.S. keep 310,000 troops on the other side of the Atlantic to help defend Western Europe from the threat of Soviet aggression? . . .

In the last test of strength on this issue, in September [1973], the Administration barely defeated an amendment calling for a 40 per cent reduction in U.S. forces overseas. A new battle is considered inevitable in the months ahead. Senator Mike Mansfield (Dem.), of Montana, intends to introduce an amendment—probably attached to the defense budget—calling for withdrawal of 50 per cent of the American forces in Europe over a three-year period.

The Senate Majority Leader insists that there is no need for a large "American expeditionary force" in Europe 29 years after World War II. In his view, the European defense picture has been changed fundamentally by the impact of the U.S.-Soviet *détente*, deep internal Russian problems, the Moscow-Peking conflict, and the striking economic recovery of U.S. allies in Europe.

Senator Mansfield told "U.S. News & World Report": "A regimental combat team in Berlin would be enough symbolically to demonstrate the American nuclear commitment to the defense of Europe."

The bulk of the American forces on the Continent, he argues, could be brought back to the U.S. and demobilized. He claims that this would not undermine the security of Western Europe, yet it would make possible a saving of most of the 17 billion dollars a year now being spent on maintaining these forces overseas.

Such arguments are strongly challenged by the Pentagon, . . . and by virtually all European political leaders.

Why is a substantial U.S. military force considered indispensable in Western Europe 29 years after World War II? Two main reasons are given by supporters:

1. It serves as evidence of the U.S. nuclear commitment to Western Europe's security. As long as a considerable number of American troops are stationed there, Soviet

military planners must calculate that virtually any military thrust into West Europe would involve the prohibitive risk of nuclear war with the U.S.

2. The American forces—four and two-thirds Army divisions—comprise a major part of the conventional fighting strength of NATO—the North Atlantic Treaty Organization. These conventional forces, it is generally conceded, could not defeat an all-out Soviet attack. Their role essentially is to deal with limited Soviet incursions, to hold an attack long enough for diplomatic exchanges to get under way and, finally, to convince the Russians that a quick conventional attack cannot succeed before running the risk of triggering nuclear war.

U.S. Defense Secretary James R. Schlesinger maintains that NATO's conventional strength is even more important than in past years when America possessed overwhelming nuclear superiority. He makes this point:

"Now, as the Soviet Union reaches nuclear parity with the United States, deterrence will be strongly reinforced if there is a balance of conventional as well as of nuclear forces. . . . Thus, a strong conventional capability is more than ever necessary—not because we wish to wage conventional war, but because we do not wish to wage any war." . . .

Actually, negotiations are in progress between NATO and the Warsaw Pact for mutual reduction of forces. Official observers say there is a possibility of an agreement that could lead to the withdrawal of between 20,000 and 30,000 U.S. troops from Western Europe over the next year in exchange for a comparable withdrawal of Soviet troops from Eastern Europe. Yet most political observers doubt that a U.S. troop withdrawal of such limited extent would satisfy Senator Mansfield and his supporters. They are demanding large-scale cuts—at least 100,000.[3]

---

[3] From "Time for Pullback in Europe?", U.S. News & World Report, April 1, 1974, pp. 15–17. Copyright 1974 U.S. News & World Report, Inc. Reprinted from "U.S. News & World Report."

Examine the map showing NATO countries and the Warsaw Pact with Figure 5–1 comparing NATO and Warsaw Pact forces in Europe. Considering this information, along with the arguments put forth by defenders and opponents of United States forces in Europe, what would you do if you were president of the United States?

1. I would immediately recall all American forces from Europe.
2. I would withdraw most American forces from Europe, leaving only a small token force to symbolize our commitment to NATO.
3. I would make a substantial cut-back in American forces and watch to see if the Russians would follow my lead.
4. I would maintain United States forces at their present level until negotiations with the Warsaw Pact produced an agreement for mutual force reductions.
5. I would increase American forces to balance the superior military strength of the Warsaw Pact.
6. I would _____. (Suggest your own alternative if you would not do any of the above.)

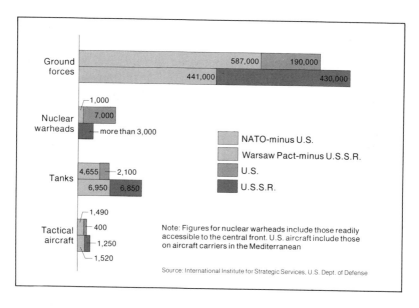

Figure 5-1. *Comparison of NATO and Warsaw Pact forces in Europe.*

NATO and Warsaw Pact Countries

NOTE: France withdrew from NATO militarily in April 1967, but remained a member politically.

AMERICAN IMPERIALISM?

One of the most persistent charges made by critics of American foreign policy since World War II is that the United States is an "imperialist" country which dominates weaker nations by its overwhelming wealth and power. Critics point to the alliances the United States has made with dozens of other countries, to the presence of American military forces around the globe, and to various interventions by the United States in the affairs of other countries as evidence of American desire to run the world. Foreign nations often look with alarm at the degree to which their businesses and industries are controlled by giant American-based "multinational" corporations. Often, when a government unfriendly to the United States is overthrown in a revolt, there are charges that the secretive American Central Intelligence Agency (CIA) has been at work behind the scenes. In 1974, for example, it was revealed that secret funds were funneled through the CIA to help bring about the unrest that resulted in the overthrow of President Salvador Allende, a Marxist who had been elected to leadership in Chile.

Critics claim that, while the United States talks a lot about democracy and freedom, it does not have any real commitment to these ideals. They believe it is hypocritical of the United States to condemn Russia for its domination of the "satellite countries" of Eastern Europe while treating its own Latin American neighbors as satellites of the United States. In Guatemala during the mid-fifties, the United States, through the CIA, aided in the overthrow of the democratically-elected government of Jacobo Arbenz. Jacobo Arbenz was considered by the American government to be an ally of the Communists. Ten years later, U.S. Marines were sent into the Dominican Republic to prevent another "Communist takeover." Many people suspected that the real motive behind these interventions was the protection of American corporations whose business interests dominated the economies of those countries.

Shortly after World War II the United States granted independence to the Philippines. In the 1950s Alaska and Hawaii were admitted to statehood, and Puerto Rico was made a "commonwealth" of the United States with its own elected government. Yet many individuals criticized the United States for holding on to several other territories like the Panama Canal Zone, where Panamanians frequently demonstrated against the American occupation of a strip of land that cuts the country in two.

Defenders of American policy see things very differently. According to their view, Americans dutifully, but reluctantly, accepted the position of world leadership that was thrust upon them after World War II. Far from seeking to dominate the world, Americans have generously provided massive quantities of economic and military aid to save other countries from Communist takeover. For the same reason, tens of thousands of Americans sacrificed their lives in Korea and Vietnam. Supporters of American policy point out that all of the alliances involving the United States are "defensive" and are designed to protect the independence of their members. They say American allies freely entered these agreements, and they are free to withdraw. Investments by American business bolster the economies of the countries in which they operate and provide jobs and tax revenues that would not exist without American capital. As for the CIA, the United States must "fight fire with fire." The Communists use espionage and secretive methods to subvert the cause of freedom. No matter how distasteful these methods may be to America's own democratic traditions, the United States is forced to resort to the same tactics.

This controversy over "American imperialism" has much to do with the situation just after World War II when the vast European empires in Africa and Asia began to break up. After the war there were millions of people in these areas who were no longer content to have their territories governed as European colonies. Like the United States in 1776, they demanded independence and were willing to fight for their freedom. Often they were supported, and sometimes led, by Communists. The European countries that claimed ownership of these territories were, in general, allies of the United States. They were the participants in the Marshall Plan, the members of NATO, and the backbone of the containment policy. The United States faced a dilemma. Should this country support these movements for independence and risk the unity of its alliance with Europe? Or should it stick by the principles stated in its own Declaration of Independence and take the chance that communism would continue to spread in the face of a disunited West?

Rightly or wrongly, American policy in the decade following World War II generally operated in favor of the European allies. The United States provided extensive aid to France in its effort to maintain control over Indochina. When the French were defeated, the Americans took their place. Similarly, the United States gave aid to the Dutch in their unsuccessful attempt to hold on to their prewar empire in Indonesia. Various votes in the United Nations on issues of colonialism showed the United States taking the side of the European imperialists.

At home and abroad people have seen two faces of America as it has played out its role on the stage of international affairs. In 1955 Prime Minister U Nu of Burma, a country that won its independence from Britain almost two centuries after the United States had done the same, delivered an address to the Overseas Press Club in New York. In his speech he summarized the reasons why people in other parts of the world both admire and fear the United States.

What do Asians think of Americans? . . .

As is only to be expected, Asians hold all sorts of views about Americans. These range all the way from those who think the Americans are heroes, brave men and women, whose mission is to make the world happier for all, to those who see Americans as a race of warmongers, spoiling for a fight, and ready to doom the world to an atomic holocaust.

Those who think of the Americans as heroes do so because of your history, your experience, your traditions, and your devotion to the principles of freedom and democracy. America was the source of those ideas and moral principles of government that have been the inspiration and hope of Asia for more than half a century. Among them are the following:

1. All men are created equal and must be equal before the law.
2. All men are endowed with certain inalienable rights which it is wrong and immoral of any government to deny or curtail.
3. A right and moral government is a government of the people, by the people, for the people, devoted to the greatest good of the greatest number.
4. A right and moral government is a government of laws, not of men, which derives its just powers from the consent of the governed.

These are tremendous ideas. They are more explosive, more powerful in their effects upon world history than all the weapons in all the arsenals. . . . These ideas played a leading part in inspiring Asia's fight for freedom from colonial bondage.

Nor is this the only reason why Asians think well of Americans. Your glorious record in the two world wars in which you undoubtedly saved the world from tyranny . . . cannot be ignored or belittled even by your most severe critics; and finally your post-World War II record, in which you have given so much of your substance to help the war-devastated countries to recover and to rebuild their shattered economies is entirely without precedent in the annals of history.

With such an impressive record behind you, it is not a matter of surprise that you should have so many admirers in Asia. Indeed the surprising thing is that there should be anyone in Asia who is dubious about America and Americans. But unfortunately there are such people, and I would like to go into the reasons for their attitude.

One very important reason for this attitude is the equivocal [ambiguous or uncertain] position which you seem to have taken in recent years on colonial issues. To an Asia which had come to regard America as the symbol of freedom, the spearhead of the attack against colonialism, and the champion of the underdog, this has indeed been not only a disappointment, but even a great shock. Some Asians have begun to wonder whether you had abandoned your heritage and your traditions. . . . When, therefore, Asians see America compromising on this fundamental question they can hardly be blamed if they begin to think that the American philosophy may have undergone a change, and to wonder whether freedom has the same meaning in America today as it had for your founding fathers.

A second reason is similar to the first. . . . Not only has America been regarded in the past as the champion of freedom; she was also regarded as the champion of democracy throughout the world. It is therefore something of a surprise to those who put their faith in democracy . . . when they see this great country allying itself with, and giving support to, regimes which by no stretch of the imagination can be regarded as "governments of the people, for the people, by the people. . . ."

A third source of misunderstanding between America and Asia stems from the activities and statements of some of your leaders, and a portion of your press. These are the people who are responsible for building the impressions abroad that America is a land of warmongers, thirsting for another war regardless of its consequences. . . . Just as some Americans talk with some justifiable pride about the tallest and biggest buildings in the world, others talk about having the biggest and latest hydrogen bombs, the fastest and largest jet bombers; and they often round off the story by giving a vivid account of what these new weapons might be capable of doing in the way of destruction on some named target in a foreign country. This has created the most unfortunate impressions in the minds of some Asians.

I personally do not believe that Americans are warmongers. You have far too much to lose to want to risk a war. I wish I could say that all Asians, or even all Burmans, feel as I do. Unfortunately, I cannot.

We all know what lies behind these apparent deviations from the American tradition. It is your preoccupation with communism. But this is something that we in Asia just do not understand. The United States today is the most powerful country in the world. It also has one of the highest standards of living. It has earned the esteem and gratitude of the people of the world for having twice in one generation saved them from fascist tyranny. Over the years, it has earned the esteem and the good will of all people who value freedom and the democratic way of life. These are all solid assets. In fact, I would say that no nation in the history of the world has occupied the predominant position which the United States occupies today.

That is why I am constantly surprised that the United States tends to exaggerate its fear of the menace of communism. And when a nation becomes obsessed with fear, it is no longer quite itself. It tends to resort to expediency at the expense of principle. It tends to forget the things which help to make it great, and begins to look for some new means of preserving its greatness.

I am convinced that what is required to remove such mis-understanding as exists in Asia of the United States is for the United States to become itself, to live up to its heritage, and to the great principles which it spawned. If this is done, you will, I feel sure, not only remove all such misunderstanding, but you will be surprised at the results not only in Asia but throughout the world. . . .[1]

As the United States prepared in the 1970s to celebrate the 200th anniversary of its independence from Great Britain, many Americans took the occasion to reassess the position of this country at home and abroad. They often found themselves grappling with the same questions that U Nu of Burma raised several years earlier. Has the United States placed too much trust in weapons and not enough in the basic principles on which the country was founded? Has an obsessive fear of communism caused America to abandon its heritage? Do Americans have a right to be proud of their record of leadership in the postwar era?

What people in other parts of the world think about America is important. But, in the long run, it is probably much more important what Americans think of themselves. How do you see the record of this country's role in world affairs? In keeping with at least one great American tradition — the decision is yours!

---

[1] From *An Asian Speaks*. A collection of Speeches made by U Nu, Prime Minister of Burma, during a visit to the United States of America, June 29–July 16, 1955. Embassy of the Union of Burma, Washington, D.C., p. 21 ff.

BIBLIOGRAPHY

"Arming to Disarm in the Age of Détente," *Time*, February 11, 1974, pp. 15–24.

Baldwin, David A. *Foreign Aid and American Foreign Policy*. New York: Praeger Publishers, 1966.

Baldwin, Hanson W. "What's Needed to Defend America?" *Reader's Digest*, January 1973, pp. 150–154.

Barnaby, Frank. "The March to Oblivion." *Science Journal*, February 11, 1971.

Bloomfield, Lincoln P. "Disarmament and Arms Control." Headline Series, No. 187. *Foreign Policy Association*. February 1968.

Blumenfeld, Yorick, "Faltering Nato Alliance." *Editorial Research Reports*, Vol. I, No. 12 (March 22, 1974).

Bottome, Edgar M. *The Balance of Terror: A Guide to the Arms Race*. Boston: Beacon Press, 1971.

Campbell, John Franklin. *The Foreign Affairs Fudge Factory*. New York: Basic Books, 1971.

Dreier, John C., ed. *The Alliance for Progress, Problems and Perspectives*. Baltimore: The Johns Hopkins University Press, 1962.

Dulles, Foster Rhea. *America's Rise to World Power, 1898–1954*. New York: Harper & Row, Publishers, 1954.

Freeman, Orville L. *World Without Hunger*. New York: Praeger Publishers, 1968.

Fulbright, J. William, *The Crippled Giant, American Foreign Policy and Its Domestic Consequences*. New York: Random House, 1972.

Gordon, Lincoln. *A New Deal for Latin America: The Alliance for Progress*. Cambridge, Mass.: Harvard University Press, 1963.

Halle, Louis J. "Does War Have a Future?" *Foreign Affairs*, October 1973.

Harriman, W. Averell. *America and Russia in a Changing World*. Garden City, New York: Doubleday & Co., 1971.

Hubbell, John G. "Shall We Build This Superbomber?" *Reader's Digest*, December 1972, pp. 121–125.

Johnson, Lyndon Baines. *The Choices We Face*. New York: Bantam Books, 1969.

Kennan, George F. *Realities of American Foreign Policy*. New York: W. W. Norton & Company, 1966.

Lappe, Frances Moore. "The World Food Problem—Natural Causation, Economic Imbalance, or Overpopulation?" *Commonweal*, February 8, 1974, pp. 457–459.

McLaughlin, Martin M. "Feeding the Unfed—The Urgency of Establishing a World Food Policy, *Commonweal*, July 12, 1974, pp. 376–379.

Murphy, Charles J. V. "The Menace of Russia's Military Machine." *Reader's Digest*, December 1973, pp. 99–103.

"NATO needs a Fresh Breeze." *Fortune*, February 1974, pp. 105–117.

Neuhaus, Richard J. "The Politics of Hunger—Manifesto on the Scandal of Global Poverty." *Commonweal*, February 8, 1974, pp. 460–463.

Paul, Roland A. *American Military Commitments Abroad.* New Brunswick, N.J.: Rutgers University Press, 1973.

Pusey, Merlo J. *The U.S.A. Astride the Globe.* Boston: Houghton Mifflin Company, 1971.

Raymond, Jack. *Power at the Pentagon.* New York: Harper & Row, Publishers, 1964.

Rostow, W. W. *The United States in the World Arena.* New York: Simon and Schuster, 1969.

Schaetzel, J. Robert. "We Mustn't Let the U.S. and Europe Drift Apart." *Reader's Digest*, March 1973, pp. 205–210.

Scoville, Herbert, Jr. "A New Arms Race Ahead?" *The New Republic*, January 19, 1974.

Shaffer, Helen B. "Nuclear Balance of Terror: 25 Years After Alamogordo." *Editorial Research Reports*, Vol. II, No. 1 (July 1970).

Steel, Ronald. *Pax Americana.* New York: The Viking Press, 1967.

Thayer, George. *The War Business: The International Trade in Armaments.* New York: Simon and Schuster, 1969.

Thurmond, Strom. *The Faith We Have Not Kept.* San Diego, Calif.: Viewpoint Books, 1968.

Ward, Barbara. *The Lopsided World.* New York: W. W. Norton & Company, 1968.

Zelnick, C. Robert. "Waiting for Disarmament: Weapons We Can Live With and Without." *Current*, August 1973.